THE TRAUMA TRAP

THE TRAUMA TRAP

Dr David Muss

Doubleday

LONDON · NEW YORK · TORONTO · SYDNEY · AUCKLAND

TRANSWORLD PUBLISHERS LTD
61–63 Uxbridge Road, London W5 5SA

TRANSWORLD PUBLISHERS (AUSTRALIA) PTY LTD
15–23 Helles Avenue, Moorebank, NSW 2170

TRANSWORLD PUBLISHERS (NZ) LTD
Cnr Moselle and Waipareira Aves,
Henderson, Auckland

Published 1991 by Doubleday
a division of Transworld Publishers Ltd
Copyright © David Muss 1991

A catalogue record for this book
is available from the British Library
ISBN 0–385–40240–6 Csd
ISBN 0–385–40241–4 Pbk

Typeset in 13/15 Bembo by
Falcon Typographic Art Ltd, Edinburgh & London
Printed in Great Britain by
Guernsey Press Co Ltd, Guernsey, Channel Islands

Contents

Tables

I dedicate this book to my wife and to all those like her who have survived PTSD for so long with so little help.

Acknowledgements

I would like to thank Margaret Hickey for her invaluable help in compiling this book and for interviewing my PTSD patients.

Likewise, I wish to thank my PTSD patients for agreeing so keenly to share their experiences in order that others may benefit through them.

I would like to thank Janice Collett, my secretary, for extending her working hours well beyond the call of duty, and putting up so cheerfully with all the chaos.

PREFACE

I have written this self-help book because I want to reach out to the vast number of people suffering from post-traumatic stress disorder (PTSD). Many of them will never had heard the name before but know something is wrong with them. They will recognize the symptoms outlined in this book.

Post-traumatic stress disorder is a condition which sets in following a traumatic event which the sufferer cannot cope with. I am not talking about an everyday sort of event which causes pain and suffering, such as the death of someone you have loved, but an event which is outside the range of usual human experience – one which is experienced in a markedly distressing way, with intense fear, terror, bewilderment and a sense of helplessness.

Examples of traumatic events which spring to

1

mind are the large-scale disasters which have occurred in the last few years: the capsize of the Zeebrugge ferry; the terrible disasters involving football spectators at Bradford, the Heysel Stadium and Hillsborough; the fires on board the Piper Alpha oil rig and the aeroplane on the runway at Manchester airport; the PanAm jet which exploded over Lockerbie, as well as the thousands of casualties caused by the Falklands campaign and the war in the Gulf.

These are well publicized examples of traumatic events which are horrific and involved large numbers of people. But, although they cause less of a sensation, the stories that never reach the headlines can devastate lives just as much. A fatal accident involving a lorry and a passenger car may only make page five of the local newspaper, but that disaster is every bit as horrifying to the people involved as one which is spread over the front pages of the national press.

Once the event is over, the reaction sets in, although in quite a number of cases the reaction is delayed. Since people are generally expected to recover from a bad experience within a few weeks, sufferers may find that support and sympathy begin to disappear when they are still feeling very distressed. At that stage they may decide to seek assistance from a professional. Very often, they try to treat themselves.

Fear of reawakening painful memories is one of the principal reasons for avoiding treatment and this is often compounded by a fear of appearing weak and out of control. Sometimes sufferers manage to reach some sort of balance in their lives, but the odds are that they are damaging themselves and those around them.

This book has been written for a variety of people. You don't have to be a victim of PTSD yourself or, indeed, have any connection with it – you may simply be intrigued by the workings of the human mind and how people react in the face of great adversity. But it is more likely that you know or suspect that PTSD is affecting your life. What I have written is also intended as a guide for the family and friends of sufferers and for people who have been caught up in a traumatic event either as bystanders or because coming to the rescue is part of their job. But it is intended particularly for all those sufferers who have not had the courage to seek treatment or who do not believe they can be helped.

As you read the book, you will come across a number of case histories. These are the stories of people who have come to me for treatment, seldom daring to hope for much and hardly ever believing they would be able to make a permanent escape from the nightmare world in which they were living. I have chosen these particular cases because they illustrate a certain aspect of the disorder or because the people involved represent different sectors of society.

People who can benefit from the book are those who:

- do not know where to turn for help;

- feel unable to let people close to them know what happened;

- were never approached after a traumatic event by a sympathetic member of society;

- felt that they could deal with all the after-effects of the trauma on their own and have discovered that they can't;

- are afraid to go for treatment in case evoking the memory will be too painful;

- fear that no treatment can help them and they may never get rid of their problem;

- are afraid to seek treatment lest they be made to feel silly or are told to pull themselves together;

- are afraid to go for treatment in case people find out and it jeopardizes their jobs;

- entered therapy and then pulled out;

- can see the sense of nipping a potential problem in the bud and want to use the treatment if they suspect they are heading for PTSD;

- want to get better without using drugs or having psychotherapy.

This book explains exactly what the symptoms of post-traumatic stress disorder (PTSD) really are and proposes a treatment which I have used successfully with many patients. I hope that those who read it with open minds will be able to return to living full lives in society, set free from the trap they may have lived in for years.

NOTE
The 'rewind technique' is mentioned in many of the case histories. This may tempt you to cut straight to Chapter 7, where the technique is explained in detail. Resist the temptation if you can. You will gain a fuller understanding of PTSD if you read the book in sequence.

DAVID MUSS
May 1991

1

WHY I BECAME INVOLVED

Many people have asked me how I came to treat post-traumatic stress disorder. The answer is simply that I became involved on a personal level.

One afternoon, seventeen years ago, I was asked to go to the telephone at the outpatients clinic of a hospital where I was working as a junior doctor. At first I couldn't recognize who it was on the other end. Then I realized it was my wife – we had been married only four months before – and her voice was tremulous and frightened. I couldn't make out what she was saying, so I rushed home (at the time we were living in the hospital grounds) to find her sitting in a heap in the centre of the living-room, sobbing. Two CID policemen were present and I learned that while she was out walking the dog in the hospital grounds she had been raped by a man who had threatened to kill her with a brick if she didn't co-operate. My own sense of shock was immense, as was an immediate sense of anger and despair.

The days that followed were horrendous. There were the ordeals of police investigations, identifying the rapist and, eventually, the court case.

After the horror, a few weeks on, when life seemed to have recovered a semblance of normality, I came home to find my wife sitting in the kitchen looking blank and shaking. Living in the same hospital grounds had become too much for her and preyed heavily on her mind. The situation was not helped by the fact that the rapist was out on bail while awaiting trial and was roaming around the hospital grounds again.

We made our decision, packed our bags and left the hospital in the next few days. I signed on the dole and we went to live with my in-laws. Our lives as a couple and my professional life had been altered dramatically by this traumatic episode.

As the months went by, although my wife began to feel stronger and started to act normally in a social way, her interest in sex had radically changed and she started to have nightmares.

These were what scared me most, as it was just like being present at the assault. She would start off by twitching a few muscles, then tossing and turning, and finally screaming out. The words at times were incomprehensible and at others clear and chilling. During that time I was training in heart surgery and had really no experience in psychology. Nor did we inform the family doctor at my in-laws, since my wife felt that he couldn't do anything for her.

The nightmares have recurred regularly throughout all these years, but now they happen perhaps once or twice a year, as opposed to once or twice a week.

My career took me into general practice, where I found that an enormous number of people were suffering from stresses of one sort or another. Unhappy with prescribing drugs, I attended an introductory course on hypnotherapy. I was impressed with its simplicity and effectiveness, and after completing an advanced course I proceeded to start group sessions at my surgery to help people relax and adopt a positive attitude.

My wife, to my dismay, would not allow herself to be hypnotized and secretly I felt that in any case I really didn't know how to deal with the nightmares through hypnosis.

My quest for a treatment of some kind that could inactivate my wife's recurring images led me to read about post-traumatic stress in the different medical books and journals. There seemed to be well over 200 articles on the subject. The majority, however, related to the effects that the Vietnam war had had on the soldiers who returned – an enormous amount of case history material had been recorded. Fewer articles referred to accidents, such as forest fires, buildings suddenly collapsing, hijacks, and the like. Now more than

900 articles have been published in medical journals, so PTSD is beginning to be recognized as a major issue.

It became apparent to us, however, that there wasn't one single type of treatment we could set off and use to achieve a rapid cure. Treatments varied from one centre to another. Many hospitals tried psychotherapy and this usually consisted of asking the patient to recall repeatedly the event which brought on the trauma until the patient could speak about it more freely. Other hospitals combined drugs with psychotherapy, and other centres tried hypnosis.

All centres reported a certain amount of success, but it was not possible to predict from the start of the treatment what type of patient would get better, or even how long it would take. The lucky ones might get better after three to twelve months of continuous treatment, while others have taken years, and many haven't got better at all.

In an article published in the *British Medical Journal* in 1988, Professor Beverley Raphael, Professor of Psychiatry at the University of Queensland in Australia, and Warwick Middleton, staff psychiatrist at the Royal Brisbane Hospital, described post-traumatic stress very neatly and pointed out how much was known about the cause of the condition and yet how little could be done to help the victims. The article called for a concerted effort to find new treatments to help patients.

I hope that the treatment I have developed, which is fully explained in Chapter 7, is the response to that call. I know that it has worked for every patient I have dealt with so far, without exception. I also have particular faith in it because I used it on myself. I arrived at this treatment too late to offer it to my wife – she felt that after eighteen years she was at last in control. If she hadn't been, I would not have been able to tell you about her in this book. But I can tell you about my own experience.

Last year, I went to Bulgaria on a skiing holiday with my children. It was one of those years when the snow had decided to make itself scarce and most of the slopes were covered with ice. I had, in fact, only skied a few times before, and my children were far more competent than I was, but, nevertheless, the accident I had didn't occur while I was skiing but while I was going up to the top of the slope on a button lift. These button lifts are actually quite awkward. They are long metal poles with a round button seat on the end of them, attached to a cable. As the cable is winched up the mountainside, the pole comes round and you have to grab hold of one and half-sit, half-ski up the slope. It is difficult enough even to catch them and sit on them, but it requires a lot of expertise to go up an icy track.

This particular button lift cable was intended to take skiers up to another, higher cable, so there were no skiers on either side of it. The children had gone on ahead of me and I was managing quite well until I got halfway up the slope. At that point my skis started sliding a bit to the left and a bit to the right and suddenly I found myself flying up into the air, losing my ski poles and landing on the icy slope. It soon became very apparent I wasn't going to stop there and I started gaining momentum downhill. In fact, I don't think I've ever gone downhill so fast on skis as I did just sliding in my ski clothes over the ice.

The nasty part was that on the left there were other skiers coming up and on the right were exposed rocks and rough terrain. Trying as hard as I could, I was unable to stop myself in any way, and the speed I was gaining was quite terrifying. My goggles came off, my watch came off and my clothes failed to halt my descent.

Suddenly, I managed to see where I was going and realized that in a few seconds I would go straight into a cable pole – one of those tall metal structures that hold up the cables. Such was my fright and the vision I had of collision and death that I curled up into a little ball. Doing that must have saved my life, because it caused me to rotate, avoiding the pole, and eventually I came to a standstill.

After a few seconds I started to shake and cry. I felt just like a lost baby, and then I had to compose myself as rescuers arrived. My first preoccupation was for the children. Where were they? After that, I just shook and shook until I was taken down to safety.

Since I had been treating other people who had been through very frightening episodes, I felt that

I ought to apply the same treatment to myself as I had to others, and I did so with very gratifying success. I don't intend to go into the details of the treatment at this point, but I can report that I was able to enjoy the rest of my holiday, and the good news is that nowadays I can talk about the event and don't get tense about it. I can also ride on a button lift without fear, and enjoy skiing as much as ever I did.

THE BIRMINGHAM–MALAGA FLIGHT

The case of Veronica Isherwood provides another illustration of the sort of event that can lead a victim into the trauma trap.

Mrs Isherwood was involved in an incident which may well be familiar to you because it hit the headlines of the newspapers and was reported on the television.

In June 1990, she was one of the eighty-one passengers on board a British Airways flight from Birmingham airport bound for Malaga. It was a fine day and Mrs Isherwood, who had frequently flown abroad in the past, was looking forward to her holiday. After about twenty minutes in the air she heard a loud bang from the front of the aircraft and, although she was seated too far back to see into the cockpit, she saw the door fly open and what she thought was smoke coming from inside.

At the same time, the plane began rocking violently from side to side. This meant she was able to see into the cockpit, where she was shocked to see the pilot being sucked out through the window, with the rest of the crew holding on to his legs.

The plane suddenly dropped (it was later discovered that it plummeted 8,000 feet) and no one knew what was happening because there was no announcement. Most people were very quiet and it seemed to her that everyone was praying. She believed at this point that there had been an explosion on board and she was going to die.

Just as abruptly, the plane came out of its nosedive and levelled out. A stewardess came running down the aisle, very distressed, telling passengers that the pilot was dead and that there would be an emergency landing at Southampton airport. In fact, the landing went smoothly and the passengers made their exit by the normal routes, but as she got off Mrs Isherwood looked round and saw what she believed was the dead body of the pilot hanging out of the cockpit window.

As you may recall, the pilot was not dead, but had nearly been sucked out of the aircraft when the bolts securing the windscreen had shot off. The crew had managed to hold on to him until the aircraft had landed and the captain was then taken to hospital, where he made a recovery.

Mrs Isherwood was not aware of the true story at the time and when she got to the lounge she was very shaken. She could remember little of

13

the flight to Malaga she and the other passengers were subsequently put on, but she had to be taken off in a wheelchair and during the holiday she had to take tranquillizers to help her sleep. Most of the daytime was spent reliving the event through flashbacks and through talking about it with the other passengers.

Although she did catch a flight back home three weeks later, she had been dreading it and when she got home she stayed off work for two weeks.

On the surface, she appeared fairly in control, but when she was questioned it emerged that hardly a day went by without her thinking about the trauma. She got a knotted feeling in her stomach and spent hours going over it all in her mind. Just when she thought she was forgetting it, she would meet someone who had seen her in the press or on television and the whole thing would be revived.

Mrs Isherwood is obviously suffering from PTSD. At the time of going to press, she has not yet been treated, but she has all the classic symptoms and there is no doubt she would benefit from the treatment.

2

THE HISTORY OF PTSD

We are dealing here with an under-researched area
of human illness. Post-traumatic stress disorder
(PTSD) is a condition which was defined only
recently (in 1980) in the diagnostic and statistical
manual of the American Psychiatric Association,
the DSM III, and members of the medical profession are more aware of it in some countries
than in others.

But the condition is widespread and its effects
on the individual and on society in general are
so debilitating that it deserves to be much more
widely known. Already, as we shall see later, the
legal profession has accepted it as a clinical illness,
and gradually doctors and social workers all over
the world are becoming aware that it is often at
the root of other problems they are used to dealing
with, such as depression and alcohol abuse.

WHEN DID PTSD FIRST APPEAR?

It is obvious that trauma did not come on the scene only when the DSM III manual defined the illness. People at every stage in history have the same emotions – they feel love, pain, fear and anger and react to trauma. People in the twentieth century may find it hard to accept, but our vastly superior technical knowledge does not mean that we are more sophisticated when it comes to our emotional lives. The capacity to feel pity or revenge, jealousy or melancholy, was to be found just as much among the weavers of the Middle Ages as it is among the stockbrokers and masters of industry today. History changes, civilizations advance or decline, but human emotion endures.

Since history sometimes seems like a long catalogue of disasters, we can surmise that PTSD has always been around – there but unreported. It is an illness which recognizes no distinctions of age, sex, religion, nationality, rank, degree of education or wealth, and it is impossible at this stage to predict who may suffer from it. What we do know is that between 30 and 60 per cent of people involved in a traumatic event go on to suffer from PTSD.

As Professor John Gunn, a leading British psychologist, has pointed out, you have only to watch the deterioration of Macbeth and his queen after the intensely stressful experience of killing Duncan to realize that PTSD has been around for a long time. In fact, Shakespeare's tragedies are fruitful ground for those who want to search back through literature for cases of the illness.

Many of us are lucky enough to escape the devastating experience which can cause PTSD, but such events do happen every day and always have. We shall see in later chapters what types of trauma are likely to precipitate the disorder and what sorts of people can fall victim to it. Below are some contemporary reports of traumatic events throughout history.

COMBAT

The battlefield has always been an area of extremely high risk – not only physical but also psychological – and the horror of war does not simply fade away when the battle is over. We know that war has effects which last for the lifetimes of those involved, soldier and civilian alike. There is no doubt in my mind that throughout history there have been unrecognized cases of PTSD, and very many soldiers and those caught up in war will have been sufferers.

It is evident that war affects the lives of civilians, but often the devastation for the non-combatants is of a magnitude not recognized at the time.

In this century we have been confronted by mass slaughter in the trenches during the First World War, and in the Second World War by the infernal concentration camps and the mass graves

17

of innocent victims of the Final Solution. Images of the children of Vietnam burned by napalm continue to remind us that war changes for ever the lives of those who have never heard of politics. Those at risk of suffering from the aftermath of war are not only the soldiers but also the civilian population at large.

War has always been reported. The doings of kings and emperors were chronicled when the lives of their subjects were ignored, and so we can call on many contemporary accounts.

THE SIEGE OF TROY

Here is an extract from Homer's *Iliad*. The fall of Troy is traditionally thought to have taken place in 1183 BC.

'Everywhere the dead lay motionless about the streets, in the houses and on the temple stairs which our tread had reverenced so long . . . The Greeks were dashing to the [palace] and thronging around the entrance with their shields locked together over their backs . . . To oppose them, the Trojans, on the brink of death and knowing their plight was desperate, sought to defend themselves by tearing up tiles from the roof-tops of houses . . . to use as missiles . . . Inside the palace there was sobbing and a confused and pitiful uproar. The building rang from end to end with the anguished cries of women.'

THE SACK OF CREMONA

In the days of the Roman Empire, the fact that the people of Cremona were fellow countrymen of the Roman troops did not prevent the latter from sacking the town and committing atrocities on its citizens. Tacitus, in his *Histories*, relates what can happen to civilians when a bloodthirsty army is allowed to run amok.

'Forty thousand armed men forced their way into the city . . . Neither rank nor years saved the victims from an indiscriminate orgy in which rape alternated with murder and murder with rape. Greybeards and frail old women, who had no value as loot, were dragged off to raise a laugh, but any full-grown girl or good-looking lad who crossed their path was pulled this way and that in a violent tug-of-war between the would-be captors . . . A single looter trailing a hoard of money or temple-offerings of massive gold was often cut to pieces by others who were stronger . . . in their hands they held firebrands, which, once they had got their spoil away, they wantonly flung into empty houses and rifled temples . . . There was a diversity of wild desires, differing conceptions of what was lawful and nothing barred. Cremona lasted them four days.'

THE BURNING OF MOSCOW

Many centuries later, the turmoil and horror of war remains the same. The battle of Borodino marked the last stand of the Russian army before Moscow. The staggering casualties of this battle have been described as 'the equivalent of a jumbo jet . . . crashing every three minutes from breakfast to sundown'. Not long afterwards, in 1812, came the burning of the city of Moscow to prevent it falling into the hands of Napoleon's troops. It was both an awesome sight and a catastrophe for the people of Moscow. Here is an extract from the account given by a Monsieur Labeaume, an officer in the French army.

> 'The most heart-rending scene which my imagination had ever conceived, far surpassing the saddest story in ancient or modern history, now presented itself to my eyes. The hospitals which contained more than 12,000 wounded soon began to burn. This offered a dreadful and harrowing spectacle . . . How shall I describe the confusion and tumult?'

The dead and wounded are more easily identified, because their injuries are visible, but we can only guess at how many people were psychologically scarred by what they experienced in the burning city. This is what happens in war at any time and in any place – the casualties are always far greater than we know or acknowledge.

THE COWARD AND THE DESERTER

In the more distant past, the fighting man had precious few rights and any sign that he was suffering psychological stress as a result of his experiences was interpreted as malingering, cowardice or treason. He was invariably severely punished, and often killed.

In the seventeenth and eighteenth centuries, soldiers were tortured if they were found to be 'cowards, traitors to their duty, blasphemers, troublemakers and liars'; desertion or refusal to fight meant death – by hanging or shooting or as the result of torture.

By the middle of the nineteenth century, the principal method of punishment and enforcing discipline was flogging. Whilst this was a cruel fate, it has been argued that it kept the authorities from inflicting even more severe punishments. In the Crimean War, for example, no death sentences seem to have been imposed.

Flogging was finally abolished in the British Army in 1881. This was indisputably a step forward, and yet some feared that once this lesser option was closed to the authorities the number of executions might increase. This appears not to have been the case, however, for the records of the Boer War in South Africa show few executions. This state of affairs was soon to change.

THE FIRST WORLD WAR

The situation did indeed change dramatically in what was somewhat ambiguously called the Great War.

The insane type of warfare conducted during the First World War kept men in conditions almost designed to derange them. The number of soldiers suffering from a variety of psychological disorders, PTSD prominent among them, must have been colossal.

The universal pattern was that the average soldier would break down after about 250 'combat days', so the generals kept rotating the deployment of the troops. Psychological casualty statistics would have been far greater but for the fact that the individual soldier frequently did not survive long enough to be classed as psychologically damaged. In any case, he was far more likely to be shot as a coward or a deserter.

In cases which can be traced, the numbers of executions in the British Army during the Great War were: in 1914, 4; in 1915, 55; in 1916, 95; in 1917, 104; and in 1918, 46. In the early years of the twentieth century, we might have expected a more enlightened attitude, but the evidence is that men who were displaying signs of extreme anxiety and were obviously not in control of themselves were, nevertheless, treated as criminals.

During the last two years of the war a great many of the men being court-martialled for cowardice or desertion made the point that they had been diagnosed as suffering from shell shock and treated in hospital for it. However, shell shock was a very vague term for a condition no one knew much about. One of those in command at the time, Lord Moran, did believe that it was a genuine condition – 'There were some men of stout heart who were brought to that plight by the blast of a shell which damaged their brains. These men had come out of some rending explosion with their skins intact but with dishevelled minds.'

While Lord Moran did at least acknowledge the existence of the condition, the courts were inclined to view the whole business of shell shock with a sceptical eye. One private charged with desertion told the court that his nerves had been shattered as a result of his being exposed to constant bombardment. He had been relying on a drug called 'cocoa extract' to calm him down, but when he no longer had access to it he had gone to pieces. Without being medically examined by either the board or the battalion doctor, he was shot.

Another private was said to have been in an extremely distraught condition for some time before leaving his post, but the plea for mercy was denied because it was the view of the commander that if it were granted 'the standard of courage in the British Army was likely to be lowered'. Sir Douglas Haig agreed; he is said to have written in red ink over the record of proceedings: 'How can we ever win if this plea is allowed?'

THE DAWN OF RECOGNITION

Nevertheless, even before this sorry time, a few physicians had begun to pay more attention to the condition of the troops. During the American Civil War, doctors observed states of physical and mental exhaustion, or neurasthenia, occurring in soldiers exposed to fighting. In official histories of the Crimean War, we find references by Da Costa to cases of 'irritable heart', which was described as a 'form of cardiac malady common among camp soldiers', and whose range of symptoms included phobias, nightmares and 'nervousness'.

In this century, studies have been carried out more rigorously and there is renewed interest in the effects that trauma has on the military. We now know that what those soldiers in the First World War were suffering from was not 'shell shock' but PTSD. Physicians of the day noted that soldiers were suffering from anxiety attacks, exaggerated reaction to loud noises or sudden movements, insomnia and repetitive dreams of battle – all classic symptoms of the disorder. They observed it correctly, but they failed to give it a name and to analyse what caused it.

Writing of this in 1919, F. W. Mott felt that these characteristic symptoms were caused by a lesion of the brain, most likely induced by carbon dioxide poisoning. But, when survivors of concentration camps presented similar symptoms, the diagnosis had to be revised, although for a long time the search for a physical cause continued.

BATTLE STRESS

By the 1940s, researchers had realized that the conditions known as shell shock, battle neurosis and combat fatigue all had common symptoms, with war stress acting as the psychological trigger for them. By the Second World War, the condition of being battle-shocked was recognized and soldiers could no longer be shot for what was clearly a psychological infirmity. By the end of the Second World War, half a million US soldiers had retired from battle because of battle shock and after the war was over the US authorities issued a film which dealt in a sympathetic way with the problems experienced by the GIs. Psychological injury was no longer a taboo subject.

The Korean War led to further interest in the phenomenon, but it was really the Vietnam War and the catastrophic condition in which many Vietnam veterans found themselves when they returned home that sparked off more intensive research into the problem. Studies have suggested that between 15 and 35 per cent of Vietnam veterans developed PTSD. *The National Vietnam Veterans Readjustment (NVVR) Study* has estimated that 470,000 of the 3.14 million Americans who served in Vietnam are current cases of PTSD.

THE VETERANS OF VIETNAM

One of the toughest things the Vietnam veterans had to face was that they were not returning home like conquering heroes but as villains in a war no one at home wanted to know about. Unit cohesion had been destroyed by the US Army's idea of putting each soldier on a 365-day tour of duty. The thinking behind this was that every soldier would realize that he had a set period of active combat and so could start counting off the days till he would get away from the front line. In practice, it meant that soldiers were reluctant to make friends because every day someone was leaving and someone else was arriving. Company morale never got a look in.

Ivan Hiller served as a sergeant with the US Marines in Vietnam, but when he was finally discharged at the end of the war he found he could not get away from his experiences there. His PTSD was severe and the recurring image he had was particularly poignant for a father.

He had got to know a child in Vietnam, a little girl called Kim, and most days she had come along for chocolate or chewing gum and had been a favourite of the soldiers. One day the enemy draped her with live grenades and sent her towards the soldiers. 'She was booby-trapped with the grenades and she was coming towards the perimeter fence.' He felt he had no option but to shoot her.

Once he got home after the war was over, he

suffered severely. 'I thought I was going crazy, seeing my own kids dead. That image of Kim kept coming back to me, but it was the image of my own kids. I was scared of hurting my own family.' In the end a judge made an order removing him from the family because it was felt there was a risk.

A number of studies have compared the psychological condition of Vietnam veterans with that of Israeli soldiers who have seen active combat, once they have returned to civilian life, and I shall examine the findings of these studies more closely in Chapter 10.

THE PSYCHIATRIC CASUALTIES OF THE FALKLANDS CAMPAIGN

Initial reports into the Falklands conflict seemed to uncover few psychiatric casualties, but, as is often the case, the reaction took some time to show itself and it is now clear that the war took its toll.

World in Action, a programme shown on British television in 1991, examined the whole issue of battle shock, psychological injury and PTSD. Tom Howard, a Scottish soldier who had seen action in the Falklands, told of his complete breakdown as a result of his experiences. 'I saw dead bodies, and the bodies were dead but the eyes were following me.' He could not get these out of his mind and started to look for ways to forget.

'I was drinking twenty pints a night and smoking – anything I could get my hands on – marijuana, pot, we even tried opium.' Needless to say, his efforts to drive out the images were unsuccessful and just brought more trouble in their wake. 'My marriage broke down – I lost my daughter, I lost my wife. The memories of the carnage are as fresh in my mind now as they were in 1982 and I know I'll have them until my dying day.'

I only hope that he gets to hear of the treatment I have developed. He need not be condemned to live with these nightmares for the rest of his life.

Another Falklands soldier was only nineteen years old when he fell victim to PTSD.

Anthony, a nineteen-year-old Welsh Guard, was on board the assault ship HMS *Galahad* when a bomb blast hit the compartment he was in below decks and he was thrown clear. His own injuries were minor: his hair and eyebrows were singed. But when he went back into the compartment he found the mutilated remains of his best friend, a married man with a young child.

Others had survived the blast, and so he sprang into action and helped to get them up on deck and gave them first aid. While this was going on, he could hear ammunition exploding down below and the screams of those trapped in the fire. Fewer than half the men in his unit survived. When he had done what he could for the men on deck, sustaining worse burns as a result of his rescue attempts, he rowed them ashore.

When he eventually left the Falklands, he showed no trace of his injuries, and he went about his self-imposed duty of visiting the widow and child of the friend who had died. This made him feel terrible, and all he could think at the time was that he should have been the one to die and his friend the one to survive.

He was given a presentation by the local council and this made him feel more guilty. His upset was made worse whenever the television showed footage of the Falklands conflict and especially when there was a programme devoted to the action in Bluff Cove, which is where his ship went down.

The reaction began to manifest itself in sweating and shaking and his heart began to race – he had palpitations. He suffered from insomnia and he spent nights with the intrusive, recurring images of the disaster playing in his head like a film.

At home he was irritable and could not discuss what was wrong. In the classic manner, he began to try to drown out the memories and the pain by turning to drink and was taking up to nine pints of beer and several measures of spirits a night. Instead of helping, the drink made him feel worse and he began to be sick and lose weight.

Anthony was one of the people who refused to seek help. He refused to consult an army doctor and would not attend a civilian clinic, but he did turn to a friend and confided in him. He may not have known why he was so adamant in refusing to seek help, but it is quite probable that it was a combination of fear of making matters even worse, reopening the wounds, and a macho idea that men do not need help from outsiders in solving their problems. It is just sad that he is going through unnecessary suffering, and if this book can help others avoid that it will have done its job.

THE GULF WAR

It is still too soon to assess the long-term consequences the war in the Gulf will have on soldiers from both sides, but no war is waged without trauma. Hugh McManners, a Commando captain during the Falklands conflict, predicts: 'In a war like the Gulf war, there is likely to be very large numbers of psychological casualties.' In particular, he feels there will be an enormous number of battle-shocked Iraqis – hidden victims who will have problems for decades to come.

Dr Mowaffak al Rubaie, a former medical officer with the Iraqi army, believes that the morale of the Iraqi soldiers was low and that they were confused about the objective of the war. In the current turmoil, there must be very many badly disturbed soldiers and civilians who are still having to face conflict, and, because of the massive aerial bombardment they were subjected to by Allied aircraft, many of them are likely to have nightmares of something falling from the sky.

NATURAL DISASTERS

While wars have been more consistently and better documented throughout the centuries than most other events, great natural catastrophes have also attracted attention. Great earthquakes and volcanic explosions have been recorded by historians and we may assume with confidence that these terrible events inflicted trauma on many who survived them.

One such was the outbreak of bubonic plague in London in 1665.

An eyewitness wrote: 'In my walks I had many dismal scenes before my eyes, as particularly of persons falling dead in the streets, terrible cries and shriekings of women who in their agonies would throw open their chamber windows and cry out in a dismal surprising manner; It is impossible to describe the variety of postures in which the passions of the poor people would express themselves.'

This witness has obviously been deeply marked by certain sights. 'It is scarce credible what dreadful cares happened in particular families every day, people in the rage of distemper or in the torment of their swellings which was indeed intolerable, running out of their own government, raving and distracted and often times laying violent hands upon themselves, throwing themselves out at their windows, shooting themselves, etc. Mothers murdering their own children in their lunacy, some dying of mere grief as a passion, some of mere fright and surprise without any infection at all; others frightened into idiotism and foolish distractions, some into despair and lunacy, others into melancholy madness.'

It was not only those afflicted by the bubonic plague who suffered, nor just a few tender-hearted observers. It was such a massive catastrophe, even by the standards of those hard times, that it went down in the annals as one of the most horrifying events in English history.

'London might well be said to be all in tears . . . the shrieks of women and children . . . were so frequent to be heard that it was enough to pierce the stoutest heart in the world to hear them.'

In the following year, 1666, what was to be known as the Great Fire of London swept through the city and was likewise a great calamity, especially coming hot on the heels of the plague. Those who had thought to have recovered from the catastrophe were hit by another great blow. It was reported thus by Samuel Pepys:

'We were in great trouble and disturbances at this fire, not knowing what to think of it . . . a most horrid noise the flames made, not like the fine flame of an ordinary fire. So home with a sad heart, and there find everybody discoursing and lamenting the fire.'

It has been estimated that between 30 and 59 per cent of people caught up in natural disasters may go on to develop PTSD. Take that figure and multiply it by the number of people who are closely connected to the victim and you get an idea of the ripple effect it can have on society.

MAN-MADE DISASTER

The book which listed all the calamities the world has known would indeed be a long one. Leaving aside warfare, there are still hundreds of thousands of them world-wide. I would remind you of two which affected huge numbers of people in the British Isles: the Highland Clearances in Scotland and the Great Hunger in Ireland. These exemplify calamities which were almost entirely avoidable and which failed to attract much sympathy or practical help for the victims until it was too late.

In the former disaster, thousands of Scottish families were evicted from their homes to make way for the Cheviot sheep and were forced into poverty and degradation. In the latter, during the great famine of 1840, the roadsides of Ireland were lined with the bodies of men, women and children who had died of starvation. Those who could escaped to America, never to return.

Is it possible that those who survived these terrible events escaped without ill effects? Imagine the state of the tenant farmer in the Highlands who was forced to leave his home by violent means and cast out with no means of making a living. And what state would the people who survived the famine be in when they themselves had nearly died of hunger and would have seen deaths by the hundred in the fields and roads around the country? It is certain that many would have been quite unable to deal with the trauma. We shall never know how many lives in the past were ruined by the tragic effects of PTSD.

WHAT DOES 'MAN-MADE' MEAN IN THIS CONTEXT?

Man-made disasters are those brought about by design, such as inhuman or criminal acts, or they may be accidents of the sort that involve human artefacts – car or aeroplane crashes, train collisions, boats capsizing. These accidents in turn can result from a variety of factors, ranging from sheer bad luck to incompetence or neglect. Often the nature of the disaster suggests that it stems from a number of causes. Let us look at some examples.

THE RAFT OF THE MEDUSA

The shipwreck of a boat bound for Senegal was not so very remarkable in the eighteenth century, but what followed was. A painting by Géricault in the Louvre depicts a raft and on it, in the last extremities of exhaustion, a handful of survivors from the *Medusa*.

Of the hundred and fifty on board when the ship went down, only fifteen were rescued. Of them six died, and the remaining nine, 'exhausted by the suffering to which they had so long been exposed, are stated to be entirely altered in appearance and constitution'.

What they had endured was first shipwreck and then the bitter knowledge that their fellows who had grabbed the lifeboats, forcing them on to a makeshift raft with very few provisions, had then cut the towlines and left them adrift.

The raft was horribly overcrowded and water began to lap over their legs. Some were injured, others half-mad with what they had gone through so far. 'Their consternation soon became extreme . . . Everything that was horrible took possession of their minds, all conceived their destruction to be at hand.'

Hunger and thirst set in and as some died their bodies were pushed overboard to lighten the raft. This gave others the idea of murdering the weak to make more room and spread the last provisions further – 'the constant dread of death and want of rest and food had impaired their faculties'.

Two of the survivors wrote: 'It was necessary, however, that some extreme measures should be adopted to support our miserable existence; we shudder with horror on finding ourselves under the necessity of retracing what we put in practice: we feel the pen drop from our hands, a deadly coldness freezes all our limbs and our hair stands on end.'

What they go on to relate are gruesome tales of cannibalism, 'after a deliberation at which the most horrible despair presided'.

The story of the raft of the *Medusa* is one in which a natural disaster is then followed by a series of violent actions perpetrated by desperate men. Sometimes the disaster is due almost entirely to misfortune. The sinking of the *Titanic* and the blaze which destroyed the *Hindenberg* are two which spring to mind.

DO WE RECOVER QUICKER FROM AN ACCIDENT THAN FROM A MAN-MADE DISASTER?

When an accident happens, people are expected by the rest of society to make a quicker recovery than if a crime has been committed. However, this is not necessarily sure to happen. Observers in the nineteenth century began to remark that some accident victims failed to make the recovery they had been expected to make and an explanation was sought.

In the 1880s, certain victims of train accidents were diagnosed as suffering from 'railway spine', an ill-defined condition characterized by symptoms indicating concussion and also PTSD. An investigation into the disorder was set under way but it took another hundred years before the condition was properly defined. And yet it is an illness which affects far more people than a number of physical conditions which have attracted a great deal of attention. And it is an illness which can cause acute misery not only for the sufferer, but for those around him or her.

THE OUTLOOK FOR THE FUTURE

In the past, in the absence of any effective professional treatment, people turned to prayer or to quacks and superstition. We can only guess at the unhappiness of those who suffered in silence, and that applies just as much to their bewildered families as to the victims of the illness. Much human misery can be laid at the door of PTSD. Unless sufferers find relief from it, their lives can be ruined.

Today, there is widespread interest in the illness. Psychologists and psychiatrists all over the world are inquiring into what causes it, why some people are more vulnerable to it than others, and how to treat it. But research takes time and costs money. PTSD is not the kind of illness that is as obviously life-threatening as cancer, for example, so it is never at the top of the list when it comes to allocating funds. Nevertheless, progress has been made and I hope that the technique that I have developed will stimulate further research.

3

WHAT IS PTSD?

Characteristics of PTSD

Post-traumatic stress disorder is just that – a disorder or illness which can arise after someone has experienced a traumatic event. It is not simple anxiety or depression, although some characteristics are shared. It has a very specific set of symptoms and if these are not present the person cannot be said to be suffering from the illness.

Here is is what the official manual states:

'The essential feature of this disorder is the development of characteristic symptoms following a psychologically distressing event that is outside the range of usual human experience [that is to say outside the range of such common experiences as simple bereavement, chronic illness, business losses and marital conflict]. The stressor [the cause of the stress] producing this syndrome would be markedly distressing to almost anyone and is usually experienced with intense fear, terror and helplessness.'

WHAT CONSTITUTES A TRAUMATIC EVENT?

The manual goes on to list the types of traumatic event which are the most common. I shall look at these more closely in Chapter 4. They are, in brief:

1 a serious threat to one's life or physical integrity;

2 a serious threat or harm to one's children, spouse or other close relatives and friends;

3 sudden destruction of one's home or community;

4 seeing another person who has recently been, or is being, seriously injured or killed as a result of an accident or physical violence;

5 (in some cases) learning about a serious threat or harm to a close friend or relative – for example, that one's child has been kidnapped, tortured, or killed.

RELIVING THE EVENT

The most outstanding symptom of PTSD is re-experiencing the trauma whether you wish to or not. Recurrent dreams may trouble you when you are asleep, and while you are awake you can suddenly find yourself recalling the event. In rare instances, you may behave as though you are reliving that experience, which can be frightening for anyone who is with you at the time. This reliving may last anything from a few seconds to several hours or even days. More often, the person is aware of where he or she is, but cannot block out the horrible memory of the trauma.

The memory most often takes the form of images, pictures of what happened, but it can also be in the form of sounds or even smells. For some people, it is more difficult to define – they talk of 'thoughts'. Whatever form the flashback takes, it is as though the episode were happening all over again. Even when sufferers feel they are beginning to 'forget', something can happen to remind them of the trauma and it all floods back.

AVOIDING REMINDERS

Apart from reliving the experience, another common symptom is that sufferers persistently avoid anything which can remind them of it and may even generate a type of amnesia specific to that event. Frequently, their feelings become numb: they respond to the outside world in a distant way – a phenomenon known as 'psychic numbing' or 'emotional anaesthesia'. Sufferers explain that they feel detached from other people, even those they love, and a loss of interest in sexual relations is quite common.

AROUSAL

Accompanying these symptoms are difficulties in sleeping and extreme jumpiness: many people report that the least thing startles them. Some complain of difficulties in concentrating or completing tasks and many people have noticed changes in how aggressive they are.

In mild cases, this may mean no more than that they are more irritable, but in more severe forms, particularly where survivors have actually committed acts of violence (as is the case with war veterans), there is a positive fear of losing control and this may express itself from time to time in unpredictable explosions of anger and aggressive behaviour or else in the opposite – an inability to release angry feelings.

THE SYMPTOMS

The official manual describes five main categories of factors that indicate the likely presence of PTSD.

The first factor is that the person has experienced an event which is outside the range of usual human experience and which would be markedly distressing to almost anyone, such as a serious threat to life or physical integrity; or serious threat or harm to children, spouse, or other close relatives and friends; or sudden destruction of home or community; or seeing another person who has recently been, or is being, seriously injured or killed as the result of an accident or physical violence.

The second factor is that the traumatic event is persistently re-experienced in at least one of the following ways:

1 recurrent and intrusive distressing recollections of the event (in young children, repetitive play in which themes or aspects of the trauma are expressed);

2 recurrent distressing dreams of the event;

3 suddenly acting or feeling as if the traumatic event were recurring, including a sense of reliving the experience, illusions, hallucinations, and flashback episodes, even those which occur on awakening or when intoxicated;

43

4   intense psychological distress at exposure to events which symbolize or resemble an aspect of the traumatic event, including anniversaries of the trauma;

The third factor is persistent avoidance of stimuli associated with the trauma, or a numbing of general responsiveness which was not present before the trauma. This is indicated by at least three of the following:

1   efforts to avoid thoughts or feelings associated with the trauma;

2   efforts to avoid activities or situations that arouse recollections of the trauma;

3   inability to recall an important aspect of the trauma (psychogenic amnesia);

4   a markedly diminished interest in significant activities (in young children this may be the loss of recently acquired developmental skills, such as toilet training or language skills);

5   a feeling of detachment or estrangement from others;

6   a restricted range of affection – for example, being unable to have loving feelings;

7   a sense of a foreshortened future, such as not expecting to have a career, marriage, or children, or a long life.

The fourth factor consists of persistent symptoms of increased arousal, which were not present before the trauma. These are indicated by at least two of the following:

1   difficulty falling or staying asleep;

2   irritability or outbursts of anger;

3   difficulty in concentrating;

4   excessive vigilance;

5   exaggerated startle response;

6   physiological reactivity when exposed to events that symbolize or resemble an aspect of the traumatic event (for example, a woman who was raped in a lift breaks out in a sweat when entering any lift).

The fifth factor is that the second, third and fourth factors must have lasted at least a month. It should be noted that the onset of symptoms may be considerably delayed. They may not appear until six months or much longer after the trauma, as is shown by the case of Betty Sivori.

In 1988, Mrs Sivori went to her doctor and reported having had a 'funny turn'. She had been suffering from myxoedema since the birth of one of her daughters and had been taking medication for it. Subsequently, she complained of depression.

This mother of six felt that her troubles stemmed

from the death of her father the previous year. Since then she had reached a point where she could leave the house only if someone went with her. She would get breathless just crossing the road with her daughter and when a panic attack came on she would shake, get hot and bothered and be very afraid of fainting. When I asked her what it was she was thinking about before the tightness came on, she would only say that she was afraid of fainting, but she promised to look into it more deeply over the weekend.

On the next two visits she told me about an accident she had been involved in some twenty years ago. It happened at a crossroads and since then she had always been wary of crossroads. Asked to relive the incident and then rewind, she did so without too much difficulty. On the last occasion when she came for treatment, her husband accompanied her. He said that he thought he had seen a miracle. 'We are back to where we were years ago.' They were both happy and smiling and felt that the problem had gone away.

The manual remarks that these symptoms become more intense in situations which remind the sufferers of the original trauma. For example, the sight of any kind of uniform may bring back agonizing memories for survivors of concentration camps and the symptoms they normally suffer may become more severe for some time afterwards.

More commonly, the sight of a stretch of road where a traffic accident happened is often enough to set off the symptoms in a PTSD sufferer. The whole incident comes back vividly and the sufferer can become incapacitated. A good example of this can be seen from a patient I treated fairly recently.

Mrs Mary Paterson was a police officer in her early forties when she came for treatment. She had been divorced and was newly remarried but she had been told at the station that she was being moved from her indoor job back on the beat. This totally panicked her because she had a terror of being a passenger in a car and wanted nothing to do with police cars.

The problem had first come to light in the summer of 1989 when she had a career review. The chief supervisor picked up the fact that she was terrified of being put back on the cars and tried to counsel her. He took her out in his car twice and talked about people in the police force living with acceptable levels of fear. She couldn't cope with that idea at all.

Two things were troubling her – her fear of going back on the beat and her fear of going back to the cars. It was this second fear that was really troubling her and it had come about because she had been involved in accidents three times. On the worst occasion, she was a passenger in a police car being driven round a roundabout at high speed when the driver's brakes failed and the car crashed straight into a wall. After the accident, she could not walk for five weeks, and although no one was killed she became very upset by the memory.

Around Christmas, she and her husband were late for a social engagement and her husband began to drive at full speed. It was too much for her and she broke down. Even when people drove her somewhere slowly and carefully, she was inclined to see accidents everywhere, although she still felt able to drive herself without too much distress.

After my initial assessment of her condition, she came back and tried the rewind technique. At first, she found that she had to talk it through out loud, but after that she was able to do the whole thing and managed to zip back through the rewind very quickly.

A week went by and Mrs Paterson returned for a check on her progress. On the drive back from the previous session she had noted an improvement and her husband felt she was doing very well. She had not yet been back in a police car but she was working as a controller and the idea of returning to the beat in the future no longer made her panic.

PTSD AND CHILDREN

An important point made in the manual is that the disorder can set in at any age, including during childhood. Psychologists investigating the effects the *Herald of Free Enterprise* disaster had on the survivors discovered that children as young as eight years old were suffering from the illness.

Since young children may not be able to express exactly what is wrong with them, parents or guardians who know of a traumatic event in a child's life should watch for signs of more than usual distress following it. These could indicate that the child is suffering from PTSD.

Of course, you may not be aware that a traumatic event has occurred, but if a child is behaving in a way which is noticeably different from usual it is prudent to look for the following signs:

A child may be mute or refuse to discuss the trauma.

In younger children, distressing dreams of the event may, within several weeks, change into generalized nightmares of monsters, of rescuing others, or of threats to themselves or to others.

A child may relive the trauma by play-acting it over and over again.

There may be diminished interest in activities which were once important and in people or pets which were once much loved.

There may also be a change in the child's attitude to what the future holds in store, such as not expecting to have a career or marriage.

49

Remember that the condition may not set in straight away. A delayed reaction is not at all unusual.

WHY ISN'T THE CONDITION RECOGNIZED MORE OFTEN?

The quality of help available from the medical profession varies a good deal. Those sufferers who can bear to admit that they have a problem that refuses to go away may well turn to their family doctor for help. Only too frequently this hard-pressed individual will prescribe a standard treatment for depression.

I am not criticizing the family doctor here, because quite often the symptoms bear all the hallmarks of depression. Unless the patient volunteers the information that he or she has been in a traumatic situation, the possibility that this is a case of PTSD may never cross the doctor's mind. Doctors are not mind-readers.

Indeed, the whole notion of PTSD may not be one the doctor has dealt with before. One reason is that the condition was not officially recognized until 1980. People are slow to take something new on board unless they have a reason to do so, and, although this situation is on the turn, there is still a long way to go before PTSD is widely known. However, the *Independent on Sunday* claimed in March 1990: 'Post-Traumatic Stress

Disorder (PTSD) is becoming part of the legal vocabulary.' Certainly, the importance of PTSD in legal actions may lead to the medical profession paying more attention to it. (The implications of this are considered in Chapter 10).

New concepts take time to filter through society until they reach a point where everyone is aware of them. We usually need to be involved in them somehow before they really make sense to us. The funny thing is that most people will be acquainted with a sufferer of PTSD, whether they are aware of it or not.

As the disorder becomes better known to the medical profession, the average family doctor will learn to be on the look-out for this illness. Nevertheless, unless the patient is frank, the doctor may easily diagnose something else which it resembles.

Another reason why the disorder often goes undiagnosed is that most sufferers want to avoid all enquiries concerning their traumatic experiences. They seldom volunteer information and when they are asked directly they either duck the question and talk in vague generalities or else they deny that there is a problem. The doctor or counsellor or whoever else is seeing the person professionally needs to be on the look-out for the disorder or else it can slip by unnoticed, masked by another condition. If sufferers do admit to a problem, it is usually that they can't sleep or are sleeping badly.

DOES EVERYONE EXPERIENCE THE SYMPTOMS IN THE SAME WAY?

In a word, no. We have looked at the symptoms which are classically present in the disorder, but these will vary to some degree from one individual to another in the way they manifest themselves.

FLASHBACK

Suppose we take the very common symptom of the involuntary flashback: just as you are going about your business, you find yourself invaded by images of the traumatic event. In the case of a traffic accident, it might be that you see the fateful car overtaking on a bend, another car coming in the opposite direction, the collision and then the ensuing scenes of injured people in the wreckage.

SOUND

While visual flashbacks are most common, it may be a sound that triggers off the horror for some sufferers. One survivor of the Piper Alpha disaster reported that some time afterwards, he heard a loud bang while he was in bed, and his immediate reaction was to dive under the blankets in a panic. The first sign that anything had gone wrong on board the oil rig was a loud explosion.

IMAGINATION

I also know from my own experience with patients (see my former patients' own accounts in Chapter 8) that serious cases of PTSD can set in even if the person was involved in a traumatic event only to the extent of hearing about it. The human mind is very powerful, and the products of our imaginations can be more horrifying than the real thing. In the case of these 'secondary' victims, as they are known, the flashbacks relate to scenes they have seen in their mind's eye.

DELAYED REACTIONS

'That happened months ago. It can't be what's bothering me.' This is what patients have said to me who know their lives are coming apart and can't think why. When they look into what has happened to them in the past, they may fail to pinpoint the incident which is at the root of the trouble because they believe it happened too long ago to be affecting them now.

Indeed, it may not even have seemed such an important thing at the time. One of my patients came away from a period in his life with the feeling that, on the whole, he'd enjoyed himself. One particular incident which happened during that period, however, had left its mark and, as if it had been on a slow fuse, his self-possession blew up some months later.

It is far from unusual for people to experience a delayed reaction to trauma. Michael Napier, a lawyer who specializes in disaster litigation, knows of cases in which the symptoms of distress have not become apparent until well over a year after the event which caused the illness. I myself have treated a patient who came to me ten years after the onset of PTSD.

None of us should imagine that people are perfectly well adjusted if they cope marvellously with a stressful event at the time. Almost anyone who has been bereaved will know that the full impact of the death of a loved one may not really be felt until months after the funeral. If this is so of a situation which comes well within the compass of common human experience, we need not be surprised to find it true of a traumatic situation. One of my patients provides a good illustration of this.

Shirley Platt, a store detective, was referred in the middle of 1989 by her family doctor, who had found her to be suffering from bouts of acute anxiety. Headache, nausea and a feeling of light-headedness were all experienced on a regular basis, but numerous medical investigations had shown nothing abnormal.

When she came for her first session, it turned out she had been suffering from panicky, claustrophobic feelings on and off for ten years. Her job as a store detective was stressful and she often experienced panic at work, at the theatre or in a coach – somewhere where there were a number of people and she could not easily be alone. She rarely had these panicky feelings at home, but the headaches and sickness were really beginning to get her down. 'I'm so tense. It's as if there are two people in my head. One says "You will have a bad pain" and the other one says "You won't". The bad one always wins. I can't get out of the circle, so I know I'm going to be poorly.'

These bad headaches came on about once a fortnight and the fact that she was also nervous of confined spaces meant that she was considering not flying to Malta for the family holiday she and her husband had planned.

Looking back at her past life, she managed to unearth the incident which was at the root of her problems. She was suffering from PTSD without knowing it, and she had been suppressing her feelings for all those years. The incident she identified was one when she was present at the scene of an accident and found a car on fire with people trapped inside it, screaming. Powerless to help, she was forced to stand by as five people died. Since then she has been unable to sit in the back of a car and has continued to have nightmares about it. She imagined different ways of dying and how her children might be hurt. She is frightened of dying – her brother died young – and she had told her family that if she did die she did not want to be cremated, because of the accident she had seen.

She tried out the rewind technique and managed it the second time. Some six weeks later, she returned and was very pleased with her progress. She had flown to the holiday in Malta without difficulty and had also used the rewind technique on another event which her husband thought might also be affecting her. Now she knew what to do with images that came into her mind, and she went away feeling that she could now cope with her life.

People whose defences are good do not allow themselves to acknowledge how deeply shaken they have been. They keep it a secret from people around them and they may try to keep it a secret from themselves. But they can't. They refuse to admit that there is something wrong for the principal reason that they cannot see what good will come of reviving old memories and opening up old wounds.

IT IS NEVER TOO LATE TO START TREATMENT
But the Sooner the Better

The traumatic event may have happened to you two months, six months, or even several years ago. Starting the treatment as soon after the trauma as possible is desirable. Prompt treatment can help prevent a sequence of events which can seriously and adversely affect the quality of life.

Fortunately, the majority of victims, even though untreated, somehow find their own ways of coping with the outside world. Inside, however, they are still suffering deeply. That is why it is so important to understand that even a very deep-seated case of PTSD will respond to treatment. Consider the case of Linda Scott, a police officer.

In this young woman's background was an unhappy relationship with her parents which arose when her mother left the family home and Ms Scott chose to live with her father. Later, she decided to go and live with her mother, and her father was so upset that he had refused to speak to her over the last two years.

She was living with her fiancé but of late she had been weepy, nervous and irritable and recently she had become physically ill.

Linda would have been quite happy to end her story here, believing, perhaps, that it should be enough to explain away all her symptoms. If I hadn't asked her directly 'Has anything frightening happened to you at all, over the last year or so?' the true story may never have surfaced.

In fact, she had been badly beaten up the year before, while on duty on her own. At the time, she thought she had got over it, but in the past two or three months it had started to affect her. She had bad dreams and was petrified of walking alone.

On the session following the initial diagnosis, she went into a very relaxed state and practised the rewind technique. On the next visit she felt good after it, no longer felt weepy and out of control and was making plans for a reconciliation with her father.

THOSE WHO REJECT HELP

Sufferers who admit that they need help are already part of the way along the road to recovery although, as we shall see in Chapter 6, the quality of help available varies. But there are many, many people who will not admit that they are suffering. Sometimes it is a case of protecting one's job. Sufferers know that they are not the person they once were, but are afraid to turn to any official source for help because they believe that once it becomes known that they have some kind of psychiatric disorder they risk losing their jobs.

I am not denying that in some cases this might

be so. There is still a great deal of medieval superstition around when it comes to mental illness and, although huge numbers of people suffer from some form of mental disorder at some time in their lives, it is seldom publicly acknowledged. Clinical depression is explained away as 'being overtired' or 'under the weather'. Well-meaning doctors write out sick notes diagnosing a viral infection, when the true cause of incapacity is an anxiety attack or a mild nervous breakdown.

There are other reasons why people refuse help. Some fear that they will be opening a can of worms if they go to seek any kind of psychiatric help. They are afraid that doctors may diagnose them as insane and commit them to an asylum, and they will never lead normal lives again.

Other sufferers believe that seeking psychiatric help will stigmatize them. What if people found out that they had been to see a shrink? How can they tell other people at work? Or how can they tell their friends and family? What will the neighbours think?

Others may have heard that treatment is expensive and can take years. They are not going to let themselves in for all that. Probably the majority simply kid themselves that they can find a cure or that in time the problem will eventually go away.

SOME HOME REMEDIES

Whether or not they know they are suffering from PTSD, people who know something is wrong will try to cure themselves using a variety of measures.

They will almost certainly try to avoid any place, any situation – indeed, avoid hearing any word or phrase – that will remind them of the trauma. This can lead to people living incredibly restricted and complicated lives – unable to take a certain route, unable to drive, unable to use a particular room in the house, and so on.

They may also use drink or drugs to help them drive away the memory, to numb themselves. Substance abuse, particularly alcohol abuse, is a crutch commonly used by the PTSD sufferer who refuses to acknowledge his or her problem. And, of course, it is not a crutch. It only adds to the problem and can so mask the condition that a doctor may not see what lies behind it.

They may try other ways of driving out the anxiety and the painful memories. Some people throw themselves into physical activities. 'You haven't got time to think when you're running around a squash court or playing a good hard game of football.' That is how the reasoning goes, but even if frantic team sports do offer some relief for an hour or two people can't spend their whole lives like that. The extra exercise may do them some good physically, but PTSD is an illness that simply refuses to go away.

MEDICAL PROBLEMS

Roderick Orner, a district psychologist in Lincoln, asserts that PTSD sufferers are 'less able to deal with the stresses and strains of everyday ordinary living. Over time, there is an insidious deterioration in their health and they become physically very unwell.'

When the mind is distressed, the body may well become affected. After they were exposed to sounds or sights which reminded them of their wartime experiences, Vietnam veterans were found to have immediate increases in their heartbeat, blood pressure and muscle tension. Many badly affected sufferers had hypertension or coronary heart disease. Alcoholism, of course, has its own medical implications. Endless unrelieved tension is bad for us – it's as simple as that. Theresa Morris's experience shows this up very clearly.

This woman had a complicated history involving a period of paralysis, a wrong diagnosis of multiple sclerosis, difficulties with driving and travelling on trains, and headaches at four o'clock every day while at work.

Three years before she came along for treatment, Mrs Morris had had a baby. She returned to work three months later, but instead of being put back in her old job, where she had been for six years, she was given different duties. She felt bitter about this when she thought of all her experience being thrown away, but she coped well enough.

One day she went to Pembroke with the amateur dramatic company she was involved with and spent the afternoon on the beach. When she got up to walk back to the town, she couldn't control her muscles and lurched around as though she were drunk. At the time she laughed about the incident, but it was followed by a spell of nausea and the next morning when she came to get up she found to her horror that the whole left side of her body was paralysed and her face was numb. With a small baby to look after, she was traumatized by the thought that she might become permanently immobile. After a week or so, however, the paralysis abated and she went to see a doctor. He diagnosed multiple sclerosis and so her initial shock was further compounded by this news.

She started getting bad headaches and when she went for a brain scan another doctor examined her and told her that the diagnosis had been wrong. Her headaches went away when the burden of worrying about multiple sclerosis was lifted and she had an excellent six weeks during which she felt right as rain. Then she went back to work and the headaches came back.

In addition to these, she got upset very easily, found it difficult to argue with people, couldn't face driving on motorways or in the rush hour, got panicky inside a train for fear she might miss her stop and generally felt unable to cope.

It was clear that a large part of her worries stemmed from the incident on the beach and so she tried the rewind technique on this episode and came back a week later to report on its effect. She had had only one headache in the intervening period. Others had seemed to start and then fade away before they really set in. 'I can't believe it happened so soon.' She had also been in a meeting at work the previous day and had expected to get tense but hadn't. When she started to feel tension she put the rewind technique into effect until she felt calm.

During her last consultation two weeks later, she said that she had had only one headache and that she now regularly took the train without panicking. Not only that, she had also taken the motorway when she went to Durham one day, and she said that it had been a lovely journey. She had regained her self-confidence and was a much happier person.

PTSD AND FAMILY LIFE

Irritability, aggression, apathy, depression, anxiety, loss of sexual interest – these characteristic signs of a severe underlying problem do not make the sufferer easy to live with. Partners feel that they are living with a different person from the one they originally chose. Children may find their father or mother less loving than they once were, and what started as one person's problem affects a whole family. Unless help is found, the most loving and understanding family begins to get worn down by the heavy demands of living with a PTSD sufferer and it is a sad fact that divorce is often the outcome. This issue is discussed in Chapter 10.

4

WHAT CAUSES PTSD?

While some of the events that can give rise to PTSD don't fit neatly into a single category, most of the disasters of this kind fall into three broad groups: accidental death and injury, death and injury by deliberate action, and natural disasters.

The first group, accidental death and injury, includes accidents involving all forms of transport – motor vehicles, trains, planes, ships and boats – as well as accidents occurring as a result of misfortunes such as falling, drowning, being struck by a falling object and accidental electrocution or poisoning.

The second group, death and injury by deliberate action, comprises actions designed to inflict hurt or loss. War, inevitably, comes top of the list, because it consists of aggression on a mass scale – bombing, shooting and all the other horrors. The same actions when they are done outside formal combat, as with terrorist attacks, can often be even more traumatic because they happen to people who are unprepared and vulnerable.

Of criminal activities, those which are most likely to damage the victim are crimes of violence – violence against the person, sexual offences and robbery. Other crimes which can provoke PTSD are burglary and criminal damage.

The third group, natural disasters, includes earthquakes, volcanic activity, flooding, tidal waves, fires, tornadoes, typhoons, drought, famine, epidemics and avalanches – what the insurance companies call acts of God.

ACCIDENTS

Accidents can happen anywhere, but most of those which can give rise to PTSD either involve some means of transport or happen in the home or at work.

TRANSPORT ACCIDENTS

In 1989, 5,501 people were killed in road traffic accidents in the United Kingdom, 84 on the railways and a further 113 in other forms of transport. A further 341,500 people were injured in road traffic accidents. In the United States, a massive 50,000 were killed and $3^1/2$ million injured. The chart give the total numbers of people killed on the road world-wide in 1987.

TABLE 1: INTERNATIONAL ROAD DEATHS, 1987

	Number of deaths	Deaths per 100,000 population	Pedestrian deaths per 100,000 population
United Kingdom	5,339	9.4	3.1

OTHER EEC COUNTRIES

Belgium	1,922	19.5	3.3
Denmark	698	13.6	2.7
France	10,742	19.4	2.9
Greece	1,682	16.9	4.1
Irish Republic	461	13.0	4.0
Italy	7,108	12.4	2.2
Luxemburg	68	18.4	1.9
Netherlands	1,485	10.1	1.2
Portugal	3,100	31.5	8.5
Spain	7,615	19.6	3.6
West Germany	1,441	13.0	2.8

REST OF EUROPE

Austria	1,469	19.4	3.3
Czechoslovakia	1,393	8.9	3.1
East Germany	1,531	9.2	2.9
Finland	581	11.8	2.8
Hungary	1,571	14.8	5.2
Norway	398	9.5	1.9
Poland	4,625	12.2	5.5
Sweden	787	9.4	1.7
Switzerland	904	13.8	3.1
Yugoslavia	4,526	19.3	5.9

	Number of deaths	Deaths per 100,000 population	Pedestrian deaths per 100,000 population
REST OF THE WORLD			
Australia	2,771	17.1	3.2
Canada	4,280	16.6	2.5
Japan	12,151	9.9	3.0
New Zealand	767	23.1	3.4
United States	46,386	19.5	3.4

NOTE

A low figure for the number of road deaths does not mean that road safety is well observed. For example, there were relatively few fatalities in New Zealand, but when we look at the size of its population we see that there is an unacceptably high casualty rate.

Other countries with high casualty rates are Portugal, Yugoslavia, Belgium, France, Spain and the United States of America.

If you stop and think for a moment about the implications of these statistics, you will realize that for every accident that occurs several people are involved, not just one. There is the actual victim, there are usually one or more witnesses, and there are those who come to the rescue: police, fire and ambulance personnel, as well as medical staff who are called on to help. At a conservative estimate, there will be four people, apart from the victim, involved in each accident, so that when we read of 50,000 fatal road traffic accidents in the United States we should envisage at least 200,000 people's lives being affected.

Road traffic accidents are easily overlooked as

causes of PTSD in comparison with such horrific crimes as mugging and rape. Because they are so common, they seldom receive much attention in the media unless there is a multiple pile-up on a motorway. But an everyday accident in which only a handful of people are involved is of major importance to those people and when you take into account the fact that friends, family and colleagues will also be affected the 'everyday accident' becomes something which affects a good section of society.

Take the case of Edward Green. His is a classic case because, although he was only the witness of a terrible event, his life was completely torn apart and his home life suffered greatly as a consequence.

One day Mr Green was driving home after work. Suddenly a lorry thundered past him. He saw with horror that a woman had just started to cross the road. The lorry slammed on its brakes, but too late – the woman was killed instantly.

Mr Green tried to carry on working normally, but every time he drove he began to anticipate horrific accidents at every turn. He would break out in a sweat, his heart would race uncontrollably and a dreadful sense of helplessness would overwhelm him.

He persevered for some three weeks but the horror of driving become too much for him. His whole life became a misery and his family suffered equally.

Eventually the stress became intolerable and he gave up his job. His family urged him to seek help.

ACCIDENTS IN THE HOME

In the United Kingdom in 1989 there were 4,835 fatal accidents in the home. A common cause of accidents in the home is fires – often caused by carelessly discarded cigarettes, faulty electrical equipment, blazes in the kitchen or clothes catching fire on being exposed to a flame. Also frequent are bad falls and accidents involving people slipping in the bath or shower. Sadly, victims of accidents in the home are often elderly people or children.

Where a traumatic incident happens in the home, the house can become 'poisoned' for the PTSD sufferer and he or she may have to move out. This can cause financial hardship and may be upsetting for the rest of the family.

ACCIDENTS AT WORK

Between 1988 and 1989, 730 fatal accidents and nearly 20,000 major injuries at work were reported in the United Kingdom. The real figures are likely to be even higher, since a number of injuries go unreported every year, particularly in the building trade. In the United States, the figures for 1988 show that 10,600 deaths and 1,800,000 disabling injuries happened in the workplace.

Being involved in, or witnessing, a serious accident at work can have a particularly powerful effect on your life if PTSD develops, because every day you will be returning to the place which can bring the images flooding back. People who have been in this situation have sometimes found it necessary to leave their jobs and look for work elsewhere. In some instances they have even found it necessary to train for an entirely new kind of work, because their former job triggered off the symptoms.

In Chapter 10 I consider more fully the whole business of trauma at work and what employers can do to minimize the effects of a traumatic workplace incident. But, if PTSD has already occurred, I can only urge you to treat yourself in the way I explain in Chapter 7.

DELIBERATE ACTION

COMBAT

Combat can be one of the most potent causes of PTSD. If we think only of the twentieth century, we can see very clearly how this disorder can take hold and ruin lives. Living in constant fear and physically pushed to the limits, the soldier has to contend with a requirement to appear in control and fearless. He is deprived of all normal social relations, far from family and friends and wondering how the people at home are getting on. The stresses are multiple. The sights and sounds of warfare are all acutely experienced by the combatant, whose senses have been sharpened by being always on the alert.

Soldiers suffering from shell shock in the First World War came back to a country which was disconcerted by their embarrassing displays. The flashbacks and hallucinations they experienced led them to act alarmingly in public – staggering, cringing, diving for cover at loud noises, and so on. Theirs was behaviour not suitable for heroes and they were often swept away into hospitals or nursing homes, out of the public eye. In the Second World War, many American soldiers were retired from the army before the end of hostilities because they were psychologically incapable of continuing.

The Vietnam veterans were the ones who brought the problem home to the public in a big way and the American people are more familiar with the concept of PTSD than most other nations because of the attention given to these men by the media.

After the Falklands campaign there were a few highly publicized cases but the tally of psychological injuries arising from that conflict did not become evident until some time after the end of hostilities. It is still rising as delayed cases are reported.

The Gulf war is too recently over for us to know what damage has been inflicted on Allied troops, and the continuing troubles in the Middle East augur badly for the Iraqi troops, the civilian population and other countries in the region.

CRIMINAL ACTS

Few people nowadays live totally without fear. Newspapers, radio and television report acts of violence every day, and we feel that we are living in an unpredictable, violent society. The case of Peter Watson illustrates how the threat of violence has always been very real in his profession, and how it eventually affected him personally.

This young man had been a police officer for seven years when, a few months before seeing me, he was violently assaulted. Since that time he had lost confidence in his own ability and had had persistent nightmares.

Together with a probation officer, he had been walking in an area out of his own patch when he saw two men he wanted to stop and gave chase. One lashed out at him while the other hit him from behind. As he fell to the ground, he saw what he thought was a knife and his only thought was that the man would use it. The probation officer began to chase the other one, and he was worried about her as well as himself. That was as much as he knew until he woke up in the casualty department in the local hospital.

Since the incident he had suffered a total loss of confidence. He felt that he couldn't do his job any more. Although he had been involved in a lot worse, this time it had really got to him. He admitted to having a macho image of himself and said that in the police you are not allowed to be scared. 'The more I think about it, the more I try to accept it as part of the job.' The trouble was that he couldn't.

A week later he reported feeling a little better, but a dream had been recurring in which he was on a road near his house, naked, scared, running and knocking on doors. No one answered. Then he was 'running towards a bloke with a knife, but I always wake up just before the bloke hits me with the knife'. He was asked to relax and then to try the rewind technique. He did it well.

The following week, he said that the dream had come back, but this time he had been able to wake himself up and come out of it. This made him feel marvellous and he had now reported back on duty and was on the night shift, without having any qualms.

Those who are most fearful are, understandably, those who feel least able to defend themselves against attack: elderly people, disabled people. Many women are so frightened of rape or sexual assault that they will not leave the house after dark unless accompanied, and those who live alone lock, bar and bolt all doors and windows as if expecting a siege.

Are these fears justified, and should we try to rid ourselves of them?

Here are the facts. One thing is instantly clear and that is that crime is on the rise almost everywhere in the world. One US senator recently claimed that in the United States one young black man in four can expect to be killed or wounded by a gun.

Between 1960 and 1970, the population of America increased by 13 per cent but the crime rate went up by 148 per cent.

In Europe, the picture is also bleak. In 1966 there were only six armed raids in Paris. By 1973 there were almost 600. In West Berlin, as it then was, the incidence of major crimes rose by 43 per cent between 1968 and 1973. That period, from the beginning of the sixties to the mid-seventies, was when the whole pattern shifted.

What had been seen as an American phenomenon – lawlessness, senseless vandalism, drug addiction and armed violence, linked to urban decay – became a European problem with a vengeance.

TABLE 2: NOTIFIABLE OFFENCES IN THE UK, 1989

ENGLAND AND WALES

Violence against the person	176,900
Sexual offences	29,700
Rape and attempted rape	3,300
Burglary	825,000
Robbery	33,200

SCOTLAND

Violence against the person	14,000
Sexual offences	3,100
Rape and attempted rape	500
Burglary	93,700
Robbery	4,400

NORTHERN IRELAND

Violence against the person	3,300
Sexual offences	900
Rape and attempted rape	not available
Burglary	14,700
Robbery	1,700

NOTE
Robbery is a crime against a person, as opposed to theft, which involves property only.

TABLE 3: INTERNATIONAL CRIME FIGURES

FRANCE 1987

Crimes against the person (all crimes)	152,402
Rape	3,196
Sexual offences	35,753
Burglaries	367,004
Armed robbery	6,500

ITALY 1989

Crimes against the person	125,769
Crimes of violence against the person	92,919
Violence with intent to kill or injury with violence	46,830
Violence against public morality	4,776
Violent assault	26,500
Private violence	30,118
Violent assault with intent to rape	996
Rape	1,296
Kidnaps	162

Sweden 1989

Offences against life and health	42,200
Offences against liberty and peace	35,700
Rape	1,462

New Zealand 1987

Crimes of violence or threat of violence	22,000
Sexual offences	519

Canada 1983

Attempted murder	900
Assault	125,000
Robbery	27,257
Sexual offences	13,864
Rape (1982)	2,528

TABLE 4: FBI STATISTICS FOR THE USA

Rape	1979	76,000	
	1988	92,000	37.6 per 100,000 population
Murders	1979	21,000	
	1988	20,700	8.4 per 100,000 population
Aggravated Assault/	1979	629,000	
Robbery with Violence	1988	910,000	370 per 100,000 population

TABLE 5: FIGURES FROM THE NATIONAL CRIME SURVEY OF THE BUREAU OF JUSTICE, USA

Violent Crime	4,482,000
Robbery	872,000
Rape	141,000
Assault	3,676,000

These figures include offences which were not reported to the police, the details about crime coming directly from the victims.

CRIME IN ENGLAND AND WALES

Taking the crime figures for the year between October 1989 to September 1990 in England and Wales, the police noted the following rises in violent crime:

Violence against the person	Up 4% to 182,000
Sexual offences	Up 1% to 29,000
Robbery	Up 8% to 35,000

Over the last ten years reported sexual offences have risen by 85 per cent. It is estimated that about 45 per cent of attacks are never reported.

These are the crimes which the police classify as violent, but other criminal acts can also be profoundly disturbing.

Burglary statistics show an increase of 17 per cent. In real terms, that means that 945,000 people's homes were broken into. Criminal damage is also up by 17 per cent, with 703,000 cases being reported. Theft and handling figures show 2,261,000 cases reported in England and Wales alone, a rise of 15 per cent over the previous twelve months.

There is enough evidence here to show that we are right in thinking that there is a real threat. The tables also show that the problem is an international one.

Nevertheless, it is a fact that those who feel most vulnerable are not, statistically, those most likely to get hurt. Whilst it is no consolation to the elderly widow who has been mugged to be told that she is in a lower band of probability, the people most often affected are young men between the ages of fifteen and thirty-four.

Let us examine the case of Mr Worthing.

Thomas Worthing, a married accountant in his early thirties with two children, was out one evening when he was attacked by a group of youths. They forced him to get into their car and took him to a deserted country road.

Pulling him from his car, they began beating and kicking him. They found his wallet and in it were documents giving his name, his occupation and the names of his wife and children. This gave them the opportunity for more sport, taunting and insulting him and threatening to go to his house and harm his family.

Finally, after hours of this treatment, they tied him to a tree and one youth put a gun to his head and said he was going to shoot him. Thomas Worthing begged and pleaded for his life, but the armed youth went ahead and pulled the trigger. The gun was empty, but at the moment the gun was fired the victim involuntarily wet and soiled his trousers. The youths were then bored with the game, and untied him and left him on the road. In a terrible state, Worthing made his way to a garage and called the police.

PTSD was subsequently diagnosed. He re-experienced the incident in the classic PTSD ways. He had intrusive memories of the event, nightmares, flashbacks and extreme fear upon catching sight of groups of youths. He was initially numb and withdrawn at home and he lost interest in his job. He felt generally estranged from society, said that he expected to die in the near future and showed other signs of the disorder, such as sleeping badly, jumping at the least thing and finding it difficult to concentrate. In fact, he was so disturbed by his experience that he soiled himself when called on to describe what had happened to him.

GET IT IN PERSPECTIVE

We know that in many of the world's nations crime, often allied with drunkenness and/or drug addiction, is on the increase and this gives cause for alarm to citizens who wish to lead peaceful lives. On the other hand, life is not worth living if we are constantly looking over our shoulders. We could die a thousand deaths anticipating trouble which may never come.

I have not written this section to alarm you unduly, but to make you beware of the attitude 'It can't happen to me'. If you take sensible precautions you may never become a victim of crime, and I hope you never do, but, if something distressing does happen to you, watch out for the onset of this disorder. You will recall that I treated myself straight away after a nasty incident so that I could be sure that PTSD would never have a chance to get a grip. The disorder is not officially recognized as existing until the distinctive symptoms have been present for longer than one month, but if they are upsetting you now there is every reason to nip the situation in the bud.

NATURAL DISASTERS

These are often large–scale phenomena which hit whole communities, as is the case with earthquakes or floods. When they occur, they can attract a good deal of short–term attention and offers of help, but in the long term interest falls away and the victims are left feeling abandoned.

Those who remember the terrible disaster at Aberfan, in Wales, when a slag–heap began its irresistible slide one morning and swamped a school full of young children, will recall that the world's media descended on the village eager for a story and the residents were relentlessly interviewed. When the media had had their fill they departed, and the people of Aberfan were expected to start reconstructing their lives in a place where there were almost no children left alive.

Studies have been carried out with the co-operation of people involved in such trauma with the aim of discovering whether or not people react differently when involved in a natural disaster rather than one which is man–made. Let us look at two.

The first study was conducted with the help of a group of firefighters in Australia and the second on the inhabitants of a rural community in North Carolina, in the United States, whose homes were hit by a tornado.

THE ASH WEDNESDAY BUSH FIRES

This study was based on the experiences of a group of 459 volunteer firefighters who were exposed to the Ash Wednesday bush fires in southern Australia in 1983.

These bush fires were so fierce that they burnt 2801 square kilometres of bush, grazing land, orchards, forests and national parks in South Australia. Several thousand trained firefighters, who lived around the fire-devastated area, were involved in attempting to control the blaze. This group had been exposed to the fire so much that it was thought that a number of them were at risk of developing PTSD. To investigate this possibility, a sample of 459 firefighters was surveyed four months after the fires had been put out.

It was borne in mind by the researchers that in Australia at any one time approximately 20 per cent of people in the general population have symptoms of psychiatric disorder. Generally, however, the disorder is short-lived and 75 per cent of sufferers regain their health. When it came to assessing the firefighters who had been caught up in a natural disaster, they took into account the possibility that any psychological disturbance they found might follow a similar course. If that were the case they would be dealing with distress and not a deep-seated illness. On the other hand, most of the symptoms that disaster victims show could stem from PTSD and follow a long-term course.

The 459 firefighters received a list of twelve questions designed to establish the degree of disturbance suffered by the group. Perhaps the key question was: 'Do your thoughts and feelings about the fire cut across or interfere with your life?' A recurring image which springs to mind despite yourself and which is seriously disturbing is a specific indicator of PTSD.

This questionnaire was sent to the group four months after the event, again at eleven months and again at twenty-nine months, in order to assess the long-term consequences of being caught up in the disaster. A high proportion of the group took the trouble to respond each time, to the delight of the researchers. When you think how easy it is to drop out of something – especially when it is time-consuming and unpaid and might awaken disagreeable memories – the co-operation they received shows that these people believed they were doing valuable work.

What emerged is that thirty-three of the firefighters were found to be suffering from PTSD on all three occasions. In other words, nearly two and a half years after the event they had not managed to rid themselves of the illness. Firefighters who had not been diagnosed as suffering from PTSD at the four-month stage displayed a delayed onset of the illness and these, significantly, were greater in number – ninety-three.

PROFESSIONAL HELP

Even more worrying was that, although a number of the firefighters had sought professional help since the disaster, there was no improvement in the figures at the twenty-nine-month stage. Paradoxically, when the participants were interviewed, it became clear that some of those most distressed by PTSD had, in fact, avoided treatment, fearing it would make matters worse.

ALCOHOL ABUSE AND PHYSICAL ILLNESS

The study found that a proportion of the firefighters suffering from PTSD had tried to deal with the problem by turning to alcohol – a 'solution' which is found time and time again among those who can't live with the distress of PTSD. Since alcohol becomes less effective at helping you forget your troubles, increasing doses have to be taken until you are no longer in control and have become dependent. The same downward spiral applies to smoking heavily and to drug abuse. These self-administered treatments increase susceptibility to a number of physical illnesses. True to the prediction, the researchers found an increased number of physical disorders among the Australian firefighters after the disaster.

CONCLUSIONS

The evidence from the study shows that even emergency-service personnel who are trained to deal with a natural disaster are not immune from its traumatic effects. Many of the sufferers were anxious to deny that there was anything wrong with them, and very few had sought professional help. (In the eleven months following the disaster, only 5 per cent had sought help for psychiatric problems and a further 6 per cent had mentioned the matter in passing to their family doctor.) Some had tried to prescribe solutions for themselves – mostly in the form of the bottle – but to no avail.

The study highlighted one final factor: the effects may not emerge until some months after the event which triggered them off. The delayed-onset form of the illness is the more upsetting because it hits you when other people feel you should have got over the shock and are unlikely to be as supportive as they would have been immediately after the event.

Compare the case of the Australian firefighters with that of some American tornado victims.

THE CAROLINA TORNADOES

In 1984, a series of tornadoes swept through part of South Carolina, leaving death and devastation in their wake. After the event, nearly 300 people visited the Federal Emergency Aid Center seeking help to pay for damaged property. Since people suffering from PTSD frequently fail to seek help, it was decided to call on these victims some five to eight months after the disaster, interview them and encourage them to fill in a checklist of symptoms. From the response it would be easy to see if the symptoms which indicate PTSD were present.

Of the potential interviewees, 279, mostly women, agreed to the interview. Most were married and their ages ranged between eighteen and eighty-nine years. Although 71 per cent had suffered no physical injury, 10 per cent had taken 'nerve pills' since the tornado and 19 per cent admitted increasing their alcohol intake. The number agreeing to fill in the checklist and a questionnaire was lower (only 42 per cent of those interviewed) but of those who did co-operate, when the clinical criteria for PTSD were strictly applied, 59 per cent were found to be suffering from acute PTSD.

In terms of people's lives, that meant that a very

large number of women had been suffering from a debilitating illness without anyone recognizing the fact. If it had not been for the study, they might have carried on trying to cope, never admitting that they were severely troubled.

The most frequently reported symptom was thinking of the event without wanting to, while insomnia, exaggerated response to sudden sounds or movements (jumpiness) and not being able to remember or concentrate as well as before were also very common. These symptoms occur in classic cases of PTSD, but the recurrent dreaming which is particularly noticed after exposure to armed combat and the so-called psychic numbing (a feeling of being detached and loss of interest in what was previously enjoyable) which are common in victims of man-made disasters were not prevalent here. This seems to indicate that there is a difference in the nature of reactions to natural and man-made cataclysms.

CONCLUSIONS

One important feature of the survey was that those suffering from severe PTSD were people who had less adequate support from family, friends, workmates, neighbours, and so on, than others. The highest frequency of PTSD was in victims aged over sixty-five or retired. In the next chapter, I examine who are the people most likely to be at risk of PTSD.

5

WHO CAN IT HAPPEN TO?

The most important thing is to realize that PTSD is something that anyone can suffer from. It affects people regardless of age, sex, education, position in society or any other category you can name. A healthy young man may not be able to withstand a trauma as well as an elderly widow, say, and at present no-one can predict who will cope best with the traumas which are able to provoke PTSD.

People who are involved in traumatic events such as those outlined in Chapter 4 find that society recognizes and makes allowances for the fact that they have undergone tremendous shock. When your life is threatened, or you are faced with the threat of injury or loss on a major scale, your predicament is easily recognized by other people, who have only to put themselves in your shoes to understand something of what you have gone through. People who have been involved in a well publicized tragedy can find themselves overwhelmed by sympathy and interest in the period immediately following. (We shall see later on how this sympathy runs out fairly quickly and often just when it is most needed – several months after the event.)

NOT JUST THE VICTIM

It is seldom appreciated that those directly involved are not the only ones who suffer. While survivors of major traumatic events stand a 30–60 per cent chance of developing PTSD, others may also develop the condition. Because we are inclined to look for it only in those most obviously involved, we may not see it in a whole range of people.

Let us take as an example a serious crime – the rape of a young mother. Naturally, the person most affected will be the young woman herself, who has been assaulted. But her family and friends will identify with her in her plight and may well see themselves in a similar position. Their close identification may lead to them living out the incident in their imaginations. If this takes a grip, they may discover that they cannot control it. They also contract PTSD and become caught in the trauma trap.

There may also have been witnesses, bystanders who saw something so upsetting that they were marked by it. These people, too, may go on to develop the disorder.

Then there are the rescuers. Usually, these are people in official positions whose job it is to deal with potentially traumatic events every day – in this instance, the police and the ambulance personnel. (Firemen are regularly called in to rescue people, too.)

Another group are the carers. In the case of the rape victim these would be the medical staff who treat her. Learning of what happened and seeing the state the young woman is in may affect them more severely than they realize at the time. A uniform does not make anyone immune from suffering from this illness.

Finally, the young mother may go to a counsellor to unburden herself of some of the nightmare memories she has. It is perfectly possible for a counsellor to hear things which go on to haunt him or her. PTSD can develop in people who were never directly involved with an incident; they become victims of someone else's trauma.

It is important to understand the full implications of this, so let us look more closely at the different groups named above.

FAMILY AND FRIENDS

Sometimes, by an unkind quirk of fate, witnesses of a disaster, either on the scene itself or watching the television, turn out to be friends or relations of those involved, and they will obviously be more powerfully affected than other bystanders. Lord Justice Wilberforce seems to understand this. In a recent judgement, *McLoughlin* v. *O'Brien*, he stated that for a case to succeed 'The shock must be through sight or hearing of the event or its immediate aftermath. Whether some equivalent of sight or hearing, for example through simultaneous television, would suffice may have to be considered.' His Lordship, Mr Justice Hidden, in the Hillsborough ruling, did in fact extend existing principles of foreseeable psychiatric injury to the results of television watching.

More commonly, bad news is broken to the family by the police or by a doctor, and when they hear the news they may proceed to imagine vividly how the events must have happened. (See the case of Mrs Drake in Chapter 8.)

The family of service personnel involved in combat may not see the actual event which caused the death or injury of their loved one, but intensive television coverage provides images of what happens to those in similar circumstances and this can easily feed the imaginations of those watching.

One study in New York City showed that 80 per cent of 'secondary' victims – friends, family and neighbours of the direct victims of violent crime – had increased levels of fear and anxiety. When the family or friends of a victim are affected by the trauma to the degree that they, too, develop PTSD, what would have been a bad enough situation to cope with turns into an even greater family tragedy.

The effects that living with a victim of PTSD can have on family and friends, who are not sufferers themselves, are considered in Chapter 10.

BYSTANDERS AND WITNESSES

This group of people consists mainly of those unfortunate enough to have been present at the scene of some disaster. Frequently, the disaster is a bad road traffic accident. A typical witness is the man or woman who is simply walking along the street or travelling in a car or bus. Out of the blue, there is a squeal of brakes followed by a collision. It all takes place within the space of a few moments while the onlooker is frozen with shock and horror.

Collisions between vehicles travelling at high speed can involve multiple pile-ups. Sometimes people are trapped inside vehicles or else a car catches fire and the bystander's feeling of helplessness just adds to the horror of witnessing the scene. Long after the accident, that person may still find himself or herself reliving it, thinking of it involuntarily and dreaming of it time and again.

It is not necessarily an accident on the motorway that causes most trouble. The many accidents which take place in suburban streets can be just as distressing to witness. It may be that an elderly person has been knocked down, or else a child. (In 1988, 462 children in Britain were killed in road accidents and over 45,000 were injured.) The sights and sounds will live with the witnesses long after the event and it is a fact that some witnesses do not manage to deal with them satisfactorily. They go on to suffer from PTSD.

Another group of witnesses are the ones who may have been partly caught up in the trauma and witnessed something that could easily have happened to them. Examples of this are people who were in parts of the stadiums at Heysel, Bradford or Hillsborough, away from the centre of danger. They were forced to stand by, powerless to help, yet very aware that something terrible was taking place. To compound their feelings of confusion and shock, there may have been the added anxiety that the trouble would spread and they too would be in danger.

Or consider the case of passengers in a hijacked plane. They may be in constant fear for their lives. We have read of hijackings where people have been forced to sit and do nothing while another passenger is picked out for execution. Not only are they in mortal terror, but they are forced to see terrible things happening around them yet avoid drawing attention to themselves. It may turn out that they are rescued and suffer no physical harm, but the psychological damage has been done and these are the circumstances under which PTSD can set in.

The plight of bystanders was recognized by the Disaster Working Party of the British Psychological Society in their 1990 report. 'All of those involved, including bystanders, may need support.' But there is often a big gap between what is recommended and what actually happens. Almost always, bystanders are moved along from the scene, often angrily by people accusing them of being ghoulish. If they are witnesses to an accident which may involve the courts, they may be required to give evidence before a judge at some stage in the future, which means that they are obliged to keep the memory fresh.

THE RESCUERS

When there has been a disaster such as a plane or train crash, a pile-up on the motorway or a major fire, the professional rescuers arrive on the scene. These may include doctors, nurses, firemen, ambulance personnel, paramedics and the police. Many of them are in uniform but a white coat or a firemen's helmet does not protect people from normal human feelings of shock, fear and horror at being exposed to dreadful sights.

Certainly, these professional people will have been highly trained and will be experienced, but when it comes to a disaster like that at the football ground at Hillsborough or the fire at King's Cross Station, many of these people will never have experienced anything on the same scale before. The necessity of getting on with their jobs, the urgent need to act quickly because lives are at stake and the knowledge that they cannot give in to panic may well carry them through the ordeal, but subsequently some of them risk becoming PTSD sufferers. No one has limitless resilience.

Sometimes it is the scale of the disaster that is the most upsetting feature, but this is not always the case, by any means. Among the many situations rescuers have to deal with as part of their work, a single incident may just touch one of them in a way that could not have been predicted. A certain aspect of the event can penetrate the professional façade and really reach the imagination. It may be a trivial detail to others, but because people are not machines one cannot predict what will push them too far.

When rescuers find that a certain incident has affected them to the point where they re-experience it in the form of involuntary flash-backs, dreams or hallucinations, it can affect their ability to continue doing their jobs. A fireman who has been called in to deal with a blaze may see something which horrifies him and then goes on to carry painful images of it around with him, unable to control them. These could be reactivated when he is called to the scene of another fire and, unless he gets help, he will find his efficiency impaired and may even reach the stage where he has to give up his job.

An article in the *Birmingham Post* in August 1990 reported that a psychologist studying the effects of the Lockerbie disaster found that police officers who had taken part in the recovery operation were suffering from shock brought about by the meaninglessness of the tragedy and their feelings of being powerless. Cases of PTSD were turning up twenty months after the disaster and the psychologist, Margaret Mitchell, of Glasgow University, quoted one officer as saying, 'I thought all the time about how the victims must have suffered and whether they were aware of what was happening to them. I couldn't get rid of the image of bodies and young children falling from the sky.'

The desire to appear strong and untouched by disaster is powerful among rescuers and the fact that other people look to them to be towers of strength may make it that much harder for them to admit to suffering as a result of what they have experienced at the scene of a disaster.

Writing in the *British Medical Journal* about the British Psychological Society conference held shortly after the Clapham Junction train crash, Martin Raw reported that the conference had emphasized the trauma suffered by the helpers. Emergency service staff called to the plane on the runway at Ringway airport, Manchester, cannot have been prepared for the appalling sight of part of the plane exploding and passengers trapped inside the burning fuselage. Similarly, some police officers called to the King's Cross fire disaster were so badly affected by what they had to deal with that they thought of leaving the force altogether.

THE CARERS

In the front line of caring are the ambulance personnel, who may also take part in the rescue, and then the staff in the casualty ward of the hospital.

On a daily basis, nurses and doctors are on call and expected to deal with emergencies, but the human psyche was never intended to be able to cope with one horrifying sight after another. Because of their dedication, we assume they have somehow mastered the situation and can cope with the most terrible sights without being affected. Of course, this is not so. It is true that a professional detachment is developed, and rightly so. Carers who are unable to help because they are too shocked and upset to think straight would be no good to anyone, and so medical staff find ways of concentrating on the job to be done and switch into a different mode when they are at work.

But later a reaction may set in. When the scale of the King's Cross fire disaster became clear, the staff in the casualty departments were put under enormous pressure. One anaesthetist, who was used to seeing horrific burns injuries, had to sort out which people were still alive from those being brought in by the ambulance teams. While she was performing this terrible task she coped marvellously but afterwards, at home, she collapsed in tears. The ordeal of dealing with so many bodies had overwhelmed her.

During the Falklands campaign, Stephen Hughes, an orthopaedic surgeon, worked with the troops, operating close to the front line. A full seven years later he had to give up work as a result of panic attacks. He claimed that they were more frightening than being on the battlefield. 'There, you know what the biggest risk is, and that is that you will be killed.' But what he found more alarming was the idea that he might be going insane. He was not. He was suffering from PTSD. Fortunately, he discovered a psychiatrist who was sympathetic and together they broke down the barriers which were holding in all the pain and fear. He now feels able to resume his life.

At the time of the Falklands conflict those involved in the combat were given no warning of the psychological hazards and no counselling afterwards, although the Ministry of Defence now claims that all soldiers can get 'comprehensive psychiatric aftercare'.

The King's Cross fire was different. After that particular disaster, student nurses who had been there were offered staff counselling and many accepted it, although some seemed to feel there was a stigma attached to being seen to need counselling. What the counsellors themselves experience is what we consider next.

THE COUNSELLORS

The British Psychological Society report entitled 'Psychological Effects of Disaster' makes an observation which applies to rescuers, carers and counsellors alike:

'There is now an increasing awareness of the impact of disasters on those involved as helpers. They are sometimes called the hidden victims.'

Because the role of the counsellor can be crucial in helping to prevent PTSD setting in, an entire chapter, Chapter 11, is devoted to them.

ARE SOME PEOPLE MORE LIKELY TO DEVELOP PTSD THAN OTHERS?

The short answer is that we don't know. Nothing has been proved one way or the other. But there are some indications we can look at.

THE CIRCUMSTANCES OF THE TRAUMA

Undergoing a severely traumatic event may push some people to the edge of PTSD, but certain additional factors, not especially dangerous in isolation, can conspire to push that person over the edge.

Being kidnapped is frightening enough, but if the kidnapping is carried out in a brutal fashion, if the victim is kept blindfolded or bound, if the kidnappers do not speak to the victim or speak another language and if the conditions in which the victim is kept are dirty, cold and comfortless, the whole experience will be a great deal more of a nightmare.

In a study of Vietnam veterans, researchers found that exposure to combat was not bound to lead to PTSD, but where that exposure was prolonged and combined with poor diet, physical discomfort, exhaustion, boredom and isolation, the risks were higher.

It is still too early to assess the effects of the Gulf war on the soldiers involved, but we already know that no war is fought without psychological casualties, among the civilians as well as the military on both sides.

On the side of the Allies, there were long periods of preparing for war, never being sure when they would be called on to act, and anxiety about the possibility of chemical warfare. Many, although not all, of the troops found themselves in a terrain and a climate they were totally unfamiliar with and they were aware of being in a kind of gigantic goldfish bowl, with the press and television crews from all over the world reporting on their every move.

The very fact of wearing the suits designed to protect against chemical weapons makes a difference to the mental welfare of troops. Once inside the suit, the soldier cannot hear very well, the lenses get fogged up, and he is alone with the pounding of his own heart and the sound of his own breathing. This increases anxiety levels and Professor Rick Gabriel, who has made a study of the plight of the soldier, believes that if armies have to fight in these chemical warfare suits the rates of psychological casualties will be doubled, if not trebled.

On the side of the Iraqi troops, there may have been a lack of commitment to the war and a presentiment that they were up against vastly superior weaponry. This is the view of Dr Mowaffak al Rubaie, formerly a medical officer with the Iraqi army. He saw signs of low morale among the soldiers and rejects the idea that most of them regarded the war as a jihad, a holy war.

One more group whose fate is unsure, even as I write, is the Kurdish people. The terror they are undergoing now, their lives in the balance, with men, women and children dying of disease, cold and hunger, must have already sown the seeds of this crippling illness in many of those unfortunate refugees.

THE PERSONALITY OF THE VICTIM

A study of American marines who showed signs of difficulty in adapting to society before they enlisted concluded that they were more likely to develop PTSD than their fellows. In the Australian study of firefighters exposed to bush fires, those who were introverted and neurotic also appeared more at risk. And a family history of mental illness, particularly anxiety or depression, may be present in up to two-thirds of chronic PTSD sufferers.

While these findings are based on only relatively few cases, and we should not jump to any conclusions, it seems likely that people with pre-existing difficulties will be less resilient than those who are well adjusted and controlled.

Nevertheless, a trauma may be such that it can devastate the strongest person. What is absolutely vital is to get rid of any notion that somehow victims of PTSD have brought it on themselves or that they could get over it if they would only pull themselves together.

THE SUPPORT OF FAMILY AND FRIENDS, AND SOCIAL ATTITUDES

This is a most interesting area to consider. John Donne reminded us that no man is an island and society is more than just a collection of individuals. Our mental health is greatly affected by how we are treated by other people. Where we are given love and support, we are more likely to cope with the stresses and burdens of life than if we are isolated or treated with hostility. That is how human beings are.

Susan Mejo, who specializes in psychiatric and mental health nursing in the United States, writes of the growing amount of literature which emphasizes the importance of the social support system in alleviating the impact of a stressful event: 'The more adequate a person's supportive network – family, friends and community – the better she or he is at coping and handling the stressful event. Conversely, negative or rejecting attitudes of family and society are an important factor. The blame that a rape survivor or Vietnam veteran often experiences has a deterrent effect on the process of recovery.'

She relates the case history of an eighty-four-year-old woman who had managed well until she was involved in a car accident. Her own car was written off and this loss seemed to open the floodgates to many other losses in her life. Tellingly, she concludes: 'The 84–year-old woman lived alone and had no one to talk with in order to normalize her feelings. Thus, they intensified until she entered treatment.'

Rebeka Moscarello, Assistant Professor of Psychiatry at the University of Toronto, writing of victims of sexual assault, believes that the amount of social support a person gets is 'the most important factor influencing rehabilitation'.

Now, it has been claimed that Vietnam veterans are less well adjusted than veterans of earlier wars because the American public lost sympathy with the Vietnam war. The soldiers who returned did not come home to a heroes' welcome. On the contrary, they found that people were unwilling to listen to their stories and there was a generalized sense that it had been a shameful episode that was best forgotten as quickly as possible.

In 1983, four researchers, led by F. S. Sierles, looked at a group of twenty-five American soldiers who had returned from the war, all suffering from PTSD. They found substance abuse (drink and/or drugs) in twenty-one out of the twenty-five and they also noted antisocial personality features, with aggressive, impulsive behaviour.

In direct contrast to that study, however, was one which was carried out on a group of twenty-five Israeli combat veterans, also suffering from PTSD, who had been referred to the PTSD Unit of the Israel Defence Forces Psychiatry Division. In only two cases was alcoholism suspected and there was no other evidence of substance abuse in any of the other soldiers. Moreover, there was no diagnosis of antisocial personality, and, while some aggressive behaviour was noted, it was not such that it was seen as a major problem.

The reasons for these differences can only be guessed at. It should be pointed out that alcoholism and drug abuse are less prevalent in Israel than in many societies, but it is surely significant that the Israeli troops had had a completely different experience from that of the Americans when they returned from active service. Israel is strongly supportive of its soldiers and a veteran is treated with respect, which may explain why these soldiers did not display the anger and alienation that the Vietnam veterans did.

IS SUPPORT ESSENTIAL FOR RECOVERY?

No. I do not mean to suggest that someone who is not fortunate enough to receive loving support in any great measure is not going to make a recovery. Not everyone is in a position to count on friends or family, and it would be wrong to state that this poses an insuperable obstacle to making a recovery, but it would be easier if this support could be counted on.

Nor does having the support mean that someone will get back to normal without treatment. Some of the Australian firefighters described in Chapter 5 went on to develop PTSD. Interestingly, among those who did go on to suffer from the disorder there were several who did not experience it straight away. It was suggested that after the disaster these men had used the support of their fellows in order to relieve their distress. When they realized that this alone was not going to resolve their problems, PTSD made itself felt.

CAN A POTENTIAL SUFFERER DO ANYTHING TO AVOID PTSD?

The most essential thing you can do if you fear you may be in danger is to read Chapter 6, which tells you what to do in the period immediately following the trauma. If you are convinced that you already have the disorder (and Chapter 7 will help you test out your intuition), then do as I did and catch the trauma before the trap firmly closes in on you.

6

FIRST AID

In this chapter I should like to deal with what you should do immediately after a traumatic event. From day one, there are things you can do which will make a vast difference to how you are affected by the trauma, and the sooner you take action to help yourself the better it will be for you and all concerned.

As you will remember, PTSD cannot be diagnosed as having developed until at least a month has gone by since the episode which triggered off the disorder. This is perfectly sensible, because it is common for people to experience a great many very disturbing symptoms in the period immediately following a trauma and there is no reason to be unduly alarmed by them in the early stages.

Nevertheless, you can help yourself straight after a trauma, and with the right help you should see these alarming and upsetting symptoms gradually diminish as time goes by. The victim of a trauma can go on to make a recovery without PTSD ever taking hold. It is when the symptoms persist, or start to increase at the end of a week or so, or when they appear to go away only to come back some time later that there is serious cause for concern.

DELAY

PTSD sets in when a process of healing, adjustment and acceptance fails to happen. Time is a healer for some but not for all. Some people fail to realize consciously that they have lived through a trauma – they have subconsciously covered up an experience and may go about their business quite normally for weeks, months, years even, before the impact of that experience hits them. When the reaction does come it can hit them like a bolt out of the blue, because they don't know what to attribute it to. The case of the surgeon who served in the Falklands conflict, described in Chapter 5, is a perfect illustration. His PTSD did not become apparent until seven years had gone by.

If something traumatic happens to you, don't behave as if it were nothing at all. You must treat yourself with respect and not expect to carry burdens without a murmur. If you react with the appropriate feelings at the time, they have less chance of lying hidden and festering.

DENIAL

Most people are well aware that they have been devastated by a traumatic event, but seem to make no progress toward healing. They may refuse help or deny that anyone is able to help. Nevertheless, these people should be encouraged to see what is on offer. If they are adamant that they will not talk to anyone, perhaps you could persuade them to look at this book. If their worry is based on making themselves vulnerable to other people, at least they will be able to read it in private.

Do not wait for problems to get really unbearable before you do something about them.

FIRST ACTIONS

THE BRADFORD CITY CRISIS LEAFLET

After the Bradford City fire disaster, a leaflet, 'Coping with a Major Personal Crisis', was issued to help those who had survived and the families and friends of those who had been killed. Based on guidelines devised by Prince Henry's Hospital in Australia, it contains advice on what your first reactions should be in the period immediately after the event:

COPING WITH A MAJOR PERSONAL CRISIS

Though what you have experienced is a unique and personal event, this pamphlet will help you to know how others have reacted in similar situations. It will also show how you can help normal healing to occur and how to avoid some pitfalls.

NORMAL FEELINGS AND EMOTIONS ALWAYS EXPERIENCED

FEAR
— of damage to oneself and those we love.

— of being left alone, of having to leave loved ones.

	– of 'breaking down' or 'losing control'.
	– of a similar event happening again.
HELPLESSNESS	– crises show up human powerlessness, as well as strength.
SADNESS	– for deaths, injuries and losses of every kind.
LONGING	– for all that has gone.
GUILT	– for being better off than others, i.e. being alive, not injured, having things.
	– regrets for things not done.
SHAME	– for having been exposed as helpless, 'emotional' and needing others.
	– for not having reacted as one would have wished.
ANGER	– at what has happened, at whoever caused it or allowed it to happen.
	– at the injustice and senselessness of it all.
	– at the shame and indignities.
	– at the lack of proper

understanding by others, the inefficiencies.

– WHY ME?

MEMORIES – of feelings, of loss or of love for other people in your life who have been injured or died.

LET DOWN – disappointments, which alternate with

HOPE – for the future, for better times.

Everyone has these feelings. The experience of other disasters has shown that they may be particularly intense if

– many people died

– their deaths were sudden, violent, or occurred in horrifying circumstances

– no body was recovered

– there was great dependence on the person who died

– the relationship with the person was at a difficult stage

– this stress came on top of others.

112

Nature heals through allowing these feelings to come out. This will not lead to loss of control of the mind, but stopping these feelings may lead to nervous and physical problems. Crying gives relief.

PHYSICAL AND MENTAL SENSATIONS

You may feel bodily sensations with or without the feelings described. Sometimes they are due to the crisis, even if they develop many months after the event.

Some common sensations are tiredness, sleeplessness, bad dreams, fuzziness of the mind including loss of memory and concentration, dizziness, palpitations, shakes, difficulty in breathing, choking in the throat and chest, nausea, diarrhoea, muscular tension which may lead to pain, e.g. headaches, neck and backaches, dragging in the womb, menstrual disorders, change in sexual interest.

FAMILY AND SOCIAL RELATIONSHIPS

New friendships and group bonds may come into being. On the other hand, strains in relationships may appear. The good feelings in giving and receiving may be replaced by conflict. You may feel that too little or the wrong things are offered, or that you cannot give as much as is expected. Accidents are more frequent after severe stresses. Alcohol and drug intake may increase due to the extra tensions.

THE FOLLOWING MAKE THE EVENTS AND THE FEELINGS ABOUT THEM EASIER TO BEAR

NUMBNESS

Your mind may allow the misfortune to be felt only slowly. At first you may feel numb. The event may seem unreal, like a dream, something that has not really happened. People often see this wrongly either as 'being strong', or 'uncaring'.

ACTIVITY

– To be active. To help and give to others may give some relief. However, over-activity is detrimental if it diverts attention from the help you need for yourself.

REALITY — Confronting the reality, e.g. attending funerals, inspecting losses, returning to the scene, will all help you to come to terms with the event.

GOING OVER THE EVENT — As you allow the disaster more into your mind, there is a need to **think** about it, to **talk** about it, and at night to **dream** about it over and over again. Children play and draw about the event.

SUPPORT — It is a relief to receive other people's physical and emotional support. Do not reject it. Sharing with others who have had similar experiences feels good. Barriers can break down and closer relationships develop.

PRIVACY — In order to deal with feelings, you will find it necessary at times to be alone, or just with family and close friends.

Activity and numbness (blocking of feelings) may be over-used and may delay your healing.

HEALING

Remember that the pain of the wound leads to healing. You may even come out wiser and stronger.

SOME DOS AND DON'TS

DON'T bottle up feelings. **DO** express your emotions and let your children share in the grief.

DON'T avoid talking about what happened. **DO** take every opportunity to review the experience within yourself and with others. **DO** allow yourself to be part of a group of people who care.

DON'T let your embarrassment stop you giving others the chance to talk.

DON'T expect the memories to go away – the feelings will stay with you for a long time to come.

DON'T forget that your children will experience similar feelings to yourself.

DO take time out to sleep, rest, think and be with your close family and friends.

DO express your needs clearly and honestly to family, friends and officials.

DO try to keep your lives as normal as possible after the acute grief.

DO let your children talk to you and others about their emotions and express themselves in games and drawings.

DO send your children back to school and let them keep up with their activities.

DO DRIVE MORE CAREFULLY. **DO** BE MORE CAREFUL AROUND THE HOME.

WARNING: ACCIDENTS ARE MORE COMMON AFTER SEVERE STRESSES.

WHEN TO SEEK PROFESSIONAL HELP

1 If you feel you cannot handle intense feelings or body sensations. If you feel that your emotions are not falling into place over a period of time, you feel chronic tension, confusion, emptiness or exhaustion. If you continue to have body symptoms.

2 If after a month you continue to feel numb and empty and do not have the appropriate feelings described. If you have to keep active in order not to feel.

3 If you continue to have nightmares and poor sleep.

4 If you have no person or group with whom to share your emotions and you feel the need to do so.

5 If your **relationships** seem to be suffering badly, or **sexual problems develop**.

6 If you have **accidents**
7 If you continue to **smoke, drink**, or take **drugs to excess since the event.**
8 If your **work** performance suffers.
9 If you note that those around you are particularly vulnerable or are not healing satisfactorily.
10 If as a helper you are suffering 'exhaustion'.

DO REMEMBER THAT YOU ARE BASICALLY THE SAME PERSON THAT YOU WERE BEFORE THE DISASTER. **DO REMEMBER** THAT THERE IS A LIGHT AT THE END OF THE TUNNEL. **DO REMEMBER** THAT IF YOU SUFFER TOO MUCH OR TOO LONG, HELP IS AVAILABLE.

Notice the stress it places on the need to be extra careful after you have gone through a major crisis. It is a period when you are at greater risk of being involved in an accident, because you are in an upset state and less apt to concentrate on what you are doing. The last thing you want to happen at this point in your life is to have your upset compounded by being involved in a car crash or an accident in the home.

I shall go on to suggest the sorts of people to whom you can turn in a crisis and organizations which can help you in the critical period straight after your trauma, but here is a checklist of tasks which may need to be done. Not all of them will apply to everyone, for each victim's circumstances are different, but some of these should prove useful.

CHECKLIST

1 After you have reported any crime or injury to the appropriate bodies (the police, hospital or doctor, insurance company, and so on), set about making yourself and your property clean and tidy. You should not do this before you report the matter to the authority in question because you may be destroying vital evidence.

2 Make sure that you are safe. This may mean getting locks or windows repaired if they have been broken in the course of an attack or a burglary.

3 Make sure that you are warm and have something to eat. It is easy to overlook such simple things if you are distraught.

4 Make sure that other people around you are properly looked after. If you have children or look after elderly relatives, you might feel too upset to have to be responsible for them at present. Make arrangements for someone else to care for them until you are able to cope again.

5   Make sure, too, that any animals, such as family pets, are cared for. If you can carry on looking after them yourself, it may help to get you back to your normal routine, but don't force it.

6   Contact your bank or the credit card authorities if a cheque book or credit card has been stolen.

7   If you are the person caring for a victim of a trauma, do these things on his or her behalf, and make sure that the victim's family and colleagues at work know something has happened. (You do not need to be too specific, if you feel the victim would prefer to keep the trauma private.)

THE GOOD NEIGHBOUR

In the past, it used to be common to rely on your neighbours to keep an eye on you and for them to help out in an emergency. You would, of course, be prepared to do the same for them. This is still the case in parts of Britain and a similar tradition of good neighbourliness can be found in societies all over the world. Just the same, many people would agree that urban life has broken down that old tradition of neighbourliness. In many cities, people don't even know the names of the folk next door.

If you are lucky enough to have good relations with the people in your local community, then by all means turn to them for comfort and support after a traumatic event. If you belong to a religious group you will find them ready to help and a strong faith often gives people in distress an extra source of strength and comfort.

Otherwise, you could turn to organizations set up to offer support for specific problems or to people whose job it is to counsel and advise those in need. (See pages 190–92.)

The following organizations have a number of branches around Britain, and sometimes the organization exists in other countries, too.

THE SAMARITANS

This organization can be found in a number of countries and exists to help people who are very distressed. They often advertise their services in the newspapers. 'Despairing? Lonely? Suicidal? Bereaved?' is how a typical ad might read.

The volunteers are trained to a high standard and, whilst not everyone who comes forward is suitable for the exacting role of a Samaritan, those who go on to help are very dedicated. If you telephone them, you will not be told what you should or should not do, so do not expect them to direct you to another organization. If you specifically ask them to advise you about another source of help, however, they will certainly be able to do so. Each area has its own list of other organizations which can go on to offer assistance in the longer term, and Samaritans themselves are able to offer more than just a sympathetic ear. There are many, many people who feel enormous gratitude to the Samaritans for helping them in their darkest hours. (See page 191.)

VICTIM SUPPORT

If you have been the victim of crime, Victim Support is an organization in the United Kingdom which has been set up to help you, and in the year 1989–90, its tenth anniversary, it offered help to half a million people, including a greater number of victims of serious crime than ever before.

The help it can offer is very varied – it is confidential and free and it ranges from simple emotional support to legal and financial advice. It may consist of a volunteer coming round to see you to listen to your story and give you sympathy, or you may want advice on how to claim compensation for what has happened to you. Some of the volunteers offer to go to court with the victim when a case is to be heard, because that can be a gruelling experience, while others are trained to give assistance with housing or welfare benefit problems.

If you decide you would like their help it is vital

to get in touch with them quickly (see page 192). They will make it easy for you because if they hear that you have had trouble – if you have been burgled, for instance – they will contact you. Their leaflet on burglary invites you to return their call and offers immediate practical help, such as how to get replacements for locks, windows or doors damaged by burglars. It also offers consolation and sympathy – 'Do let us know if you would like to talk to someone.'

You will recall from the figures quoted in Chapter 4 that many more crimes are committed in Britain than those listed below, which are only those cases which were actually referred to the scheme. The numbers of victims who do not receive counselling or aid from the scheme are actually much, much higher.

Referrals to the various groups around England, Wales and Northern Ireland can be broken down as follows:

Victims of burglary were by far the most frequently referred: in all they accounted for 62 per cent of all cases. Then came violent crime, which accounted for 18 per cent of all cases. Other types of crimes made up the rest.

Of course, the weight of numbers is not the only factor to take into account. Another way of looking at the situation is to see how serious the crime was. In 1989–90, victims caught in 424 cases of homicide were referred, 1,619 cases of rape, 5,897 other sexual assaults, 82,627 cases of robbery or wounding or assault, a massive

313,698 cases of burglary and more than 100,000 other cases involving a variety of crimes. For every case referred, several victims may have been involved, so we can see that in our society many people's lives are touched by crime and its repercussions.

The scheme's priority areas have been identified as follows:

1   dealing with victims of road traffic accidents;

2   examining how better to protect young men, who are statistically the most vulnerable group in our society;

3   giving more support to young homosexual men, who are often targets of violence;

4   making sure that victims of violence in the home, almost always women or children, are better protected;

5   developing a special project which focuses on children, who are often victims of unreported crimes or witnesses of serious crimes committed against adults.

MEDIA COVERAGE OF DISASTERS

The scheme is involved with a great many bodies all working to improve the lot of the victim. It has made its views felt on the way broadcasters can affect the victim of crime. Many of you reading this will know that insensitive news items can revive terrible memories, and just when you think the media has forgotten about an incident they return to it. Many victims dread the anniversaries of an event which hit the headlines, because there is every chance that the media will take the opportunity to rerun film relating to the disaster.

RAPE

RAPE CRISIS CENTRES

These can be found in all parts of the United Kingdom and in the Republic of Ireland. Each centre is autonomous; there is no central body directing them. Any woman, girl or child who has been raped or sexually assaulted, including those who have been victims of incest, can turn to these centres for help. (See pages 190–92.)

Trained volunteers operate a telephone counselling line and they offer immediate as well as continuing support, medical and legal advice, information on the procedures the rape victim is likely to come across in court and help in claiming compensation. When funds allow, there are also salaried staff who work there.

THE UNREPORTED CRIME

Rape can be devastating and no victim of rape should try to hide what has happened, although many fail to report the crime. For example, in Toronto in 1988, 2,154 sexual assaults were reported to the police. If the estimate that only a fifth of incidents are ever reported to the police is correct, that means that there were over 10,000 victims in the city of Toronto that year. As long ago as 1973, the FBI estimated that a forcible rape took place every ten minutes in the United States.

IMMEDIATE TREATMENT

How the woman is treated in the period immediately after the attack can affect the way she goes on to make a recovery. Since many women do not continue to come for treatment once the initial crisis is over, it is important that those first hours are really effective. One study has shown that only a quarter of the victims who entered an immediate post–sexual–assault programme actually completed the fourteen-hour course of therapy.

THE HYSTERIC AND THE ROBOT

In the past, reporting a rape to the authorities often seemed as great an ordeal as the assault itself. Women who were angry, anxious, emotionally unstable and disorganized in their behaviour were seen as being hysterical, but at least their state of mind was understood.

However, there is another style of presentation which victims of a major psychological trauma can adopt. The victim is cool, collected, somewhat detached and is able to recount the events leading up to the trauma in a calm and coherent fashion. When a woman displaying this type of reaction reports a violent attack, she does not fit the stereotype of the victim, and inexperienced police or medical officers may be tempted to disbelieve her. The feeling that she is not believed and is seen as a potential perjurer and trouble-maker can have very detrimental effects on a rape victim.

Psychologists know that terror of death leads to regression and this can result in a victim behaving like a robot, calm and organized. Think of the passengers and crew of a hijacked jet. The pilot cannot go to pieces because he has to carry on flying the plane, and the passengers dread drawing attention to themselves in any way, so they sit where they are and appear to be well under control, even if they fear for their lives. The same sort of behaviour is what the calm rape victim is displaying.

POLICE CENTRES

Nowadays, the dynamics of rape are better understood and in a number of areas the police have
established specialist teams trained to take over
when a rape is reported. Some police forces have
even set up their own centres where assistance is
offered by officers specially trained to deal with
the very sensitive issue of rape and sexual abuse.

RAPE WITHIN MARRIAGE

There remains one interesting aspect of crisis
intervention following rape and that is where
rape is committed within marriage. Only recently
have the courts in Britain recognized the crime
of rape within marriage, something campaigners
have been pressing for for years, and it may be
that women raped by their husbands go in the first
instance to a shelter for battered wives rather than
a rape crisis centre or to the police. The staff of
such centres are accustomed to providing help and
support for other crimes of violence and should be
on the look-out for this one, too, which women
are frequently reluctant to admit.

Chapter 9 provides a much more detailed list of
organizations which can help. Some of them are
geared to crises, but more are there to offer help

in the long term, to get your life back on an even keel. If you find that you do go on to develop PTSD, follow the treatment given in Chapter 7 and then use Chapter 8 as a guide for any other worries or difficulties you may have. Chapter 10 deals with the PTSD sufferer back in society, both in the family and back at work.

7

THE TREATMENT

As I mentioned in Chapter 2, I had a very personal reason for becoming interested in the whole business of what happens to people to whom life has dealt a heavy blow – one outside the normal range of human experience. Many people discover that they can draw on reserves they never suspected they had and find the strength to carry on. But many others are unable to do that.

Some six years ago, I became interested in something called neurolinguistic programming, more commonly referred to as NLP. The name was invented by two people, Richard Bandler and John Grinder, who take a very unusual approach to conventional psychology, although fully versed in it. In their books, they define NLP as 'an educative process' and describe many practical ways of helping people to change their behaviour and thinking patterns. They are particularly convinced that they can treat phobias very quickly.

NLP has won respect for itself and its strengths are the speed with which it can effect change and the consequent lack of stress on the part both of the client and of the counsellor, psychiatrist or psychologist working with the techniques. It was this capacity to achieve the most profound change in the shortest imaginable time that really attracted me.

In addition, I was struck by a remark in one of the books that, some six years after details of these treatments for phobias had been published, psychologists still continued to believe that it takes months or even years of therapy and drugs to cure people of their phobias. They have never, it seems, been prepared to try out the new techniques. The authors pointed out that, if these new techniques had been major technical innovations in industry, manufacturers would have been eager to try the new methods. Industrial espionage exists because industrialists know that developments are being made all the time which allow processes to be carried out more quickly and cheaply than before. They naturally want to keep up with the state of the art.

Not so the psychologists. They appear to be possessed of a certain inertia and seem suspicious of a method which claims to do in a very short time what they have traditionally taken months or years to accomplish. I began to wonder why these NLP techniques were not being tried by psychologists and psychiatrists and, because of my home situation, I was very interested in the techniques Bandler and Grinder put forward.

I decided to take up the challenge and try out the technique that they proposed, adapting it as I felt necessary. I was in a position where I had the material to work on and I knew that if my feelings were correct I might be in a position to offer fast relief to people who desperately needed some.

From that early decision, I have gone on to develop the treatment which forms the heart of this book. I have treated many people with a variety of problems and always with remarkable results. Some of their stories are recounted in Chapter 8, which gives a number of case histories.

In this chapter I shall go on to give very precise instructions, but first I think it is extremely important that you understand clearly what can be achieved through this treatment.

WHAT TO EXPECT FROM THE TREATMENT

The technique described in this book will rid you of the various involuntary, unwanted, memories of the event, such as the nightmares, the flashbacks and the dreams. As a result of this you will no longer succumb to the emotional distress which these bring about.

The technique does not cancel your voluntary recall of the event. You will always be able to remember the event if you choose to. However, when you choose to recall the event, you know you will be mostly in control of your emotions and not overpowered by them as you are now when the event is unexpectedly recalled by a chance remark from a friend or a sudden newsflash on the TV or radio. You will no longer be imprisoned in the trauma trap – you will be released from it.

It is most important that you follow the treatment exactly as I have set it out for you. Do not try to skip parts of it or rush into it without the preparation I ask you to make. I want you to benefit from my experience and I know what steps are necessary if you are to achieve the results I have achieved with my patients.

In the next few pages I shall take you through the initial steps of assessing how severe your PTSD is and preparing for the treatment day. When you have gone through these stages, the treatment follows.

Remember that it is never too late to start treatment, but the sooner you do it the better. (See page 57.)

HOW SEVERE IS YOUR PTSD?

Before I describe the self-help treatment, please fill in the questionnaire. It is called the IES (impact of events scale) questionnaire, and it is offered as a routine matter to sufferers of post-traumatic stress disorder before they begin treatment. Only then should you proceed to the treatment. In two weeks' time, fill in the identical questionnaire at the end of this chapter. The results should be strikingly different.

PREPARE FOR YOUR TREATMENT DAY

Once you summon up the courage to treat yourself, I would recommend that you make it a special occasion and choose your day carefully in order to guarantee that you will be undisturbed. You may, if you wish, choose to be accompanied by one or more people who are close to you and whom you trust.

Before getting into the technique proper, it will make things easier for you if you are in as relaxed a frame of mind as possible. You should, therefore, follow these steps to get yourself relaxed.

Find somewhere comfortable to sit for about fifteen minutes. You may feel more comfortable with your feet up and your hands unclasped. Close your eyes and start to relax each muscle

IES QUESTIONNAIRE

NAME _____

ON _____ YOU EXPERIENCED _____
(DATE)   (LIFE EVENT)

Below is a list of comments made by people after stressful life events. Please check each item, indicating how frequently these comments were true for you DURING THE PAST SEVEN DAYS. If they did not occur during that time, please mark the 'not at all' column.

FREQUENCY

	Not at all	Rarely	Sometimes	Often
1 I thought about it when I didn't mean to.				
2 I avoided letting myself get upset when I thought about it or was reminded of it.				
3 I tried to remove it from my memory.				
4 I had trouble falling asleep or staying asleep, because of pictures or thoughts about it that came into my mind.				
5 I had waves of strong feelings about it.				
6 I had dreams about it.				
7 I stayed away from reminders of it.				
8 I felt as if it hadn't happened or it wasn't real.				
9 I tried not to talk about it.				
10 Pictures about it popped into my mind.				
11 Other things kept making me think about it.				
12 I was aware that I still had a lot of feelings about it, but I didn't deal with them.				
13 I tried not to think about it.				
14 Any reminder brought back feelings about it.				
15 My feelings about it were kind of numb.				

group of your body from your feet all the way up to your head. Relaxing each group of muscles is easily done by tightening them first and then letting them go. You should specifically include the following muscle groups as you proceed from your feet up to your head.

Start by relaxing your feet and ankles. Just concentrate on these muscles, tighten them and relax them. Then relax the muscles of your calves, thighs, stomach, back and chest, shoulders, arms and hands, neck, head and face, including forehead, nose, lips and chin. Do not clench your jaw.

You will find that a pleasant overall feeling of calmness will come over you as you slowly and systematically relax all these muscle groups. Indulge in this pleasant feeling of calmness for a while and, when you are feeling truly calm, start the treatment.

THE REWIND TECHNIQUE FOR VICTIMS OF A TRAUMATIC EVENT

Please note that this section is only for survivors directly involved in a traumatic event. If you are a bystander or a rescuer, please ignore this section and go straight to the sections starting on page 148 or page 155, which are intended specially for you. Counsellors should first read Chapter 11.

The rewind technique consists of watching a

film of your traumatic event, in the exact way that it haunts you, first forwards and then backwards. However, it is not quite as simple as that and it is very important that you follow precisely all the steps described below.

Some of the things I am going to ask you to do may seem a little odd, so let's pretend that I am introducing you to a new game. As with all new games, you need to understand the rules and the setting before you play. So, before you start the treatment, learn the rules with me.

FLOATING OUT

First, learn to float out of yourself.

Another way of saying this is: learn how to *watch yourself*. Have you been on a boat or a car journey and felt terribly sick? Or have you been on a roller-coaster and felt frightened? Stop and think about this for a moment. Have you remembered what it felt like? You probably didn't enjoy that memory, did you? This is because you didn't detach yourself.

Try now to look at the same event in a detached way. Float out of the boat, leaving your body in it, and watch yourself from the shore. Do you feel as bad as you did when you saw yourself before? I hope the answer is no. This is because you are watching yourself and not reliving the event as it happened.

THE SETTING

I would now like to explain the setting.

You will be watching two films in a cinema. Let's assume that you have a completely empty cinema hired just for you. Imagine that you are sitting in the centre with the big screen in front and the projection room behind you.

Now I would like you to float out of your body and go to the projection room to *watch yourself* watching the film from there. From the projection room you will be able to see the whole cinema, the empty chairs with just your head and perhaps shoulders sitting in the centre seat, and the screen in front of you, as in Fig. 1.

Now let's consider the two films.

THE FIRST FILM

The first film is a replay of the traumatic event as you experienced it or as you remember it in your nightmares, dreams or flashbacks. In this film you will see yourself on the screen – just as if someone had unexpectedly taken a video on the day and is now showing it to you.

Run the film forwards at its normal pace and stop when your memory begins to fade.

You will find it very helpful if you can start the film a little before the point where your memory of the traumatic event begins. In other words, if you were involved in a car accident with a lorry, begin the film by seeing yourself driving along happily, as in Fig. 2.

You then see the lorry appear (Fig. 3), and finally the accident (Fig. 4). I call Fig. 2 the 'new starting-point'. It is the point you return to when you rewind the film.

So, for the forward film: first remember where you are sitting and where you are watching the film from. Then begin from the 'new starting-point'. Next, see yourself on the screen. Finally, let the film run along until your memory fades.

THE REWIND

The second film is called the rewind. You do not exactly watch the rewind. You are actually in it,

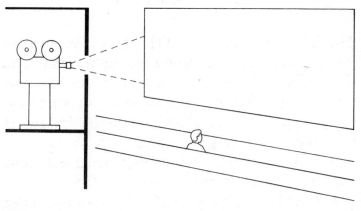

Figure 1

Figure 2

Figure 3

Figure 4

experiencing it *in* the screen, seeing everything as if it were happening to you now. The really odd thing is that you see and feel everything happening *backwards*.

Thus, in the case of the car accident, first you are *in* the car after the impact (Fig. 5). Then you feel the car pulling away from the lorry. You see the front of your car returning to its normal shape, as does the lorry (Fig. 6). The vehicles pull farther and farther apart until the lorry disappears and you finally end up with the 'new starting-point', as in Fig. 7 – you *see yourself* driving along in your car as you did at the beginning of the forward film.

Remember, in the rewind you are actually in the film, re-experiencing the event – which is now, however, all happening in reverse.

The rewind must be done rapidly. You may find this difficult at first. If so, practise it slowly to start with. When you've got it right, run it through straight after the forward film.

To give you an idea of the speed of the rewind, if the forward film takes one minute the rewind should take 10–15 seconds at the most.

You should end the rewind at your 'new starting-point', which represents a good image.

To sum up, with the forward film, you are sitting in the centre of the cinema, leaving your body there and floating to the projection room, from where you will watch the forward film. See yourself on the screen. Begin with your new starting-point. Run the first film until it fades.

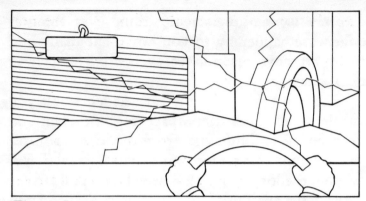

Figure 5

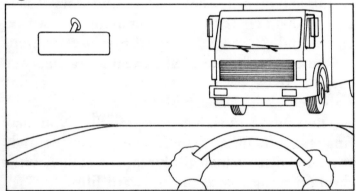

Figure 6

Figure 7

At this point get into the film. You are no longer watching the film, but re-experiencing the traumatic event in reverse. Rewind the event rapidly. End with your new starting-point.

I must warn you that going through the first film can be painful and, if a person dear to you is sitting next to you, he or she may well see you becoming pale, sweaty or even tearful. Please don't be put off, either of you. Remember that this should be the last time you remember the event in this way.

After this treatment you will find that whenever the memory is sparked off the rewind will rapidly come into play, and will, on its way back, scramble the sequence, leading you very quickly to the new starting-point. The new starting-point is a good image and that is the memory you will be left with. This process will happen faster and faster as every day goes by. As a result of this treatment, you will find that you are now able to resume all the activities which you haven't been able to do for a long time.

SOME DIFFICULTIES YOU MAY ENCOUNTER

Some people find rewinding difficult and slow to do at first. Don't be discouraged; practise the rewind on its own until you get it right. Then go through the complete sequence without hesitating or stopping.

Some people often don't have the courage to look at the film in its full detail. It is fairly common to find people wanting to gloss over the really frightening or ugly part. If you do this, you will find that your PTSD symptoms will not disappear completely. You will therefore have to go back and deal with that particular section again, and, since this will be particularly unpleasant, it makes sense to have someone close to you when you do the rewind.

A NEW MEMORY ARISES

You may be deeply shocked to find that, once you have got rid of a major haunting memory, another one appears. This shouldn't surprise you. Quite often we suppress several disturbing images and, once the major one has been removed, the next most disturbing rises to take its place. If a deeper, concealed memory surfaces, just deal with it in the same way – rewind it.

Don't overreact and think that there may be hundreds more. The greatest number I've treated in one person is four.

RESULTS OF THE REWIND TECHNIQUE

The case of Clifford Jones illustrates just what effect the rewind technique can have on a PTSD sufferer who was directly involved in a traumatic event.

Clifford Jones, a police officer, was fifty-two when he came for treatment. His wife, to whom he had been married for thirty years, was a depressive who suffered from paranoia. That put a considerable strain on him. However, Mr Jones was normally patient with his wife and knew how to handle her, even though she spent most of her time goading him. She had a nervous breakdown in 1978 and in 1987 she was sent to a mental hospital, where her condition improved on taking the tablets prescribed for her. However, after coming home she had refused to take medication.

Eighteen months before coming for treatment, Mr Jones was involved in a very serious incident in which a policeman was shot dead. Mr Jones ran towards the killers and then saw them shoot a second officer, who was seriously wounded. He himself was held at bay by the gunman for five minutes and the whole thing was terrifying and nightmarish in the extreme.

Since that event, he had suffered badly. He would wake up at four o'clock in the morning and be unable to get back to sleep. He was irritable, lacked confidence and had lost interest

IES QUESTIONNAIRE

NAME *Clifford Jones*

ON ✗ **5·7-90** YOU EXPERIENCED *Held at gun point by killer –*
(DATE)   (LIFE EVENT)

Below is a list of comments made by people after stressful life events. Please check each item, indicating how frequently these comments were true for you DURING THE PAST SEVEN DAYS. If they did not occur during that time, please mark the 'not at all' column.

FREQUENCY

	Not at all	Rarely	Sometimes	Often
1 I thought about it when I didn't mean to.	✓			
2 I avoided letting myself get upset when I thought about it or was reminded of it.			✓	
3 I tried to remove it from my memory.				✓
4 I had trouble falling asleep or staying asleep, because of pictures or thoughts about it that came into my mind.		✓		
5 I had waves of strong feelings about it.	✓			
6 I had dreams about it.	✓			
7 I stayed away from reminders of it.	✓			
8 I felt as if it hadn't happened or it wasn't real.	✓			
9 I tried not to talk about it.			✓	
10 Pictures about it popped into my mind.			✓	
11 Other things kept making me think about it.		✓		
12 I was aware that I still had a lot of feelings about it, but I didn't deal with them.	✓			
13 I tried not to think about it.		✓		
14 Any reminder brought back feelings about it.			✓	
15 My feelings about it were kind of numb.	✓			

146

in everything. He could no longer put up with his wife's taunts as he had before and lately he had hit her on two occasions, something he had never done before.

Mr Jones was taught how to do the rewind technique. He said that he recalled the event as a series of actions. He wasn't sure if he saw it all in colour or not. When he had run the film through, he had difficulty with the rewind at first, because he was going back a few steps and then running the film forwards again. He tried once more with more success and arranged to come back a week later.

On his return he reported that he had slept better and had not woken up with feelings of anxiety. He had also not thought about the incident very often.

Mr Jones's two IES questionnaires, one completed before treatment and one after, are reproduced here. They speak for themselves.

THE REWIND TECHNIQUE FOR WITNESSES

This treatment is designed for bystanders present at a traumatic event as well as for friends and relations who have seen the event unfold on television or have heard it on the radio. This section is for those people only. If you are a rescuer

IES QUESTIONNAIRE

NAME *Clifford Jones*

ON **26·7·90** YOU EXPERIENCED *Held at gun point by Killer –*
(DATE)   (LIFE EVENT)

Below is a list of comments made by people after stressful life events. Please check each item, indicating how frequently these comments were true for you DURING THE PAST SEVEN DAYS. If they did not occur during that time, please mark the 'not at all' column.

	FREQUENCY			
	Not at all	Rarely	Sometimes	Often
1 I thought about it when I didn't mean to.		✓		
2 I avoided letting myself get upset when I thought about it or was reminded of it.	✓			
3 I tried to remove it from my memory.	✓			
4 I had trouble falling asleep or staying asleep, because of pictures or thoughts about it that came into my mind.		✓		
5 I had waves of strong feelings about it.	✓			
6 I had dreams about it.	✓			
7 I stayed away from reminders of it.	✓			
8 I felt as if it hadn't happened or it wasn't real.		✓		
9 I tried not to talk about it.	✓			
10 Pictures about it popped into my mind.		✓		
11 Other things kept making me think about it.		✓		
12 I was aware that I still had a lot of feelings about it, but I didn't deal with them.		✓		
13 I tried not to think about it.	✓			
14 Any reminder brought back feelings about it.		✓		
15 My feelings about it were kind of numb.	✓			

148

or a friend or relation who has had to identify a body, please go straight to the section starting on page 155, which is intended specially for you.

The rewind technique consists of watching a film of your traumatic event, in the exact way that it haunts you, first forwards and then backwards. However, it is not quite as simple as that and it is very important that you follow precisely all the steps described below.

Some of the things I am going to ask you to do may seem a little odd, so let's pretend that I am introducing you to a new game. As with all new games, you need to understand the rules and the setting before you play. So, before you start the treatment, learn the rules with me.

FLOATING OUT

First, learn to float out of yourself.

Another way of saying this is: learn how to *watch yourself*. Have you been on a boat or a car journey and felt terribly sick? Or have you been on a roller-coaster and felt frightened? Stop and think about this for a moment. Have you remembered what it felt like? You probably didn't enjoy that memory, did you? This is because you didn't detach yourself.

Try now to look at the same event in a detached way. Float out of the boat, leaving your body in it, and watch yourself from the shore. Do you feel as bad as you did when you saw yourself before? I hope the answer is no. This is because you are watching yourself and not reliving the event as it happened.

THE SETTING

I would now like to explain the setting.

You will be watching two films in a cinema. Let's assume that you have a completely empty cinema hired just for you. Imagine that you are sitting in the centre with the big screen in front and the projection room behind you.

Now I would like you to float out of your body and go to the projection room to *watch yourself* watching the film from there. From the projection room you will be able to see the whole cinema, the empty chairs with just your head and perhaps shoulders sitting in the centre seat, and the screen in front of you, as in Fig. 8. Now let's consider the two films.

THE FIRST FILM

The first film is a replay of the traumatic event as you experienced it or as you remember it in your nightmares, dreams or flashbacks. In this film you will see yourself on the screen – just as if someone

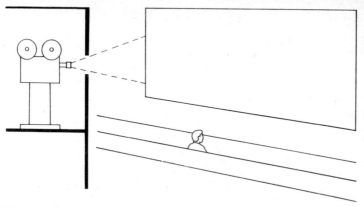

Figure 8

had unexpectedly taken a video on the day and is now showing it to you.

Run the film forwards at its normal pace and stop when your memory begins to fade.

You will find it very helpful if you can start the film a little before the point where your memory of the traumatic event begins. If your traumatic event consisted of seeing a familiar statue waver and then fall off the top of a building to the ground, breaking up into many pieces, then begin the film by seeing yourself walking along the road towards the building with the statue still looking solid, as in Fig. 9.

I call this the 'new starting-point'. It is the point you return to when you rewind the film.

So, for the forward film: first remember where you are sitting and where you are watching the film from. Then begin from the 'new starting-point', seeing yourself on the screen. Finally, let the film run along until your memory fades.

THE REWIND

The second film is called the rewind. You do not exactly watch the rewind. You are actually in it, *experiencing* it *in* the screen, seeing everything as if it were happening to you now. The really odd thing is that you will be seeing and feeling everything happening *backwards*.

Thus, in the episode of the falling statue, you will start to see the pieces come together again, the statue reform and be drawn rapidly up to its original place on top of the building as in Fig. 10 – steady as it always had been before the fall.

Remember, in the rewind you are actually in the film, re-experiencing the event, which is now, however, all happening in reverse.

The rewind must be done rapidly. You may find this difficult at first. If so, practise it slowly to start with. When you've got it right, run it through straight after the forward film.

To give you an idea of the speed of the rewind, if the forward film takes one minute the rewind should take 10–15 seconds at the most.

You should end the rewind at your 'new starting-point' (Fig. 9), which represents a good image.

To sum up, with the forward film, you are sitting in the centre of the cinema, leaving your body there and floating to the projection room, from where you will watch the forward film. See

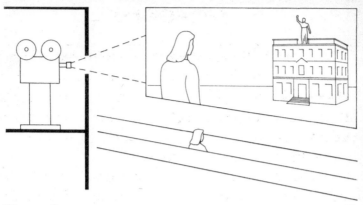

Figure 9

yourself on the screen. Begin with your new starting-point. Run the first film until it fades.

At this point get into the film. You are no longer watching the film, but re-experiencing the traumatic event in reverse. Rewind the event rapidly. End with your new starting-point.

I must warn you that going through the first film can be painful and, if a person dear to you is sitting next to you, he or she may well see you becoming pale, sweaty or even tearful. Please don't be put off, either of you. Remember that this should be the last time you will have to remember the event in this way.

After this treatment you will find that whenever the memory is sparked off the rewind will rapidly come into play, and will, on its way back, scramble the sequence, leading you very quickly to the new starting-point. The new starting-point is a good image and that is the memory you will be

Figure 10

left with. This process will happen faster and faster as every day goes by. As a result of this treatment, you will find that you are now able to resume all the activities which you haven't been able to do for a long time.

SOME DIFFICULTIES YOU MAY ENCOUNTER

Some people find rewinding difficult and slow to do at first. Don't be discouraged; practise the rewind on its own until you get it right. Then go through the complete sequence without hesitation or stopping.

Some people often don't have the courage to look at the film in its full detail. It is fairly common to find people wanting to gloss over the really frightening or ugly part. If you do this, you will find that your PTSD symptoms will not disappear completely. You will therefore have to go back and deal with that particular section again, and since this will be particularly unpleasant it makes sense to have someone close to you when you do the rewind.

A NEW MEMORY ARISES

You may be deeply shocked to find that, once you have got rid of a major haunting memory, another one appears. This shouldn't surprise you. Quite often we suppress several disturbing images and, once the major one has been removed, the next most disturbing rises to take its place. If a deeper, concealed memory surfaces, just deal with it in the same way – rewind it.

Don't overreact and think that there may be hundreds more. The greatest number I've treated in one person is four.

THE REWIND TECHNIQUE FOR RESCUERS AND RELATIONS OR FRIENDS WHO HAVE HAD TO IDENTIFY A BODY

Please note that this section is only for the people named in the heading. Victims and bystanders should refer to the appropriate sections earlier on in this chapter.

The rewind technique consists of watching a film of your traumatic event, in the exact way that it haunts you, first forwards and then backwards. However, it is not quite as simple as that and it is very important that you follow precisely all the steps described below.

Some of the things I am going to ask you to do may seem a little odd, so let's pretend that I am introducing you to a new game. As with all new games, you need to understand the rules and the setting before you play. So, before you start the treatment, learn the rules with me.

FLOATING OUT

First, learn to float out of yourself.

Another way of saying this is: learn how to *watch yourself.* Have you been on a boat or a car journey and felt terribly sick? Or have you been on a roller-coaster and felt frightened? Stop and think about this for a moment. Have you remembered what it felt like? You probably didn't enjoy that memory, did you? This is because you didn't detach yourself.

Try now to look at the same event in a detached way. Float out of the boat, leaving your body in it, and watch yourself from the shore. Do you feel as bad as you did when you saw yourself before?

I hope the answer is no. This is because you are watching yourself and not reliving the event as it happened.

THE SETTING

I would now like to explain the setting.

You will be watching two films in a cinema. Let's assume that you have a completely empty cinema hired just for you. Imagine that you are sitting in the centre with the big screen in front and the projection room behind you.

Now I would like you to float out of your body, and go to the projection room to *watch yourself* watching the film from there. From the projection room you will be able to see the whole cinema, the empty chairs with just your head and perhaps shoulders sitting in the centre seat, and the screen in front of you, as in Fig. 11. Now let's consider the two films.

THE FIRST FILM

The first film is a replay of the traumatic event as you experienced it or as you remember it in your nightmares, dreams or flashbacks. Run the film forwards at its normal pace and stop when your memory begins to fade.

157

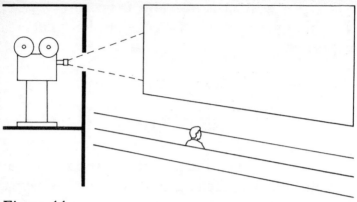

Figure 11

You will find it very helpful if you can start the film a little before the point where your memory of the traumatic event begins. Let's say that your traumatic event consisted of arriving at a scene and finding that two trains had collided (Fig. 16). Obviously, this is the first impression you get, but let's say you can imagine the trains travelling happily along before the collision, as in Fig. 12. This will be your 'new starting-point'. Then continue with the rest of the film, which may

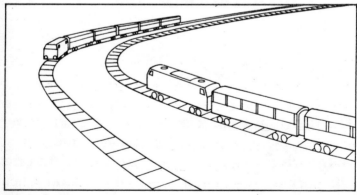

Figure 12

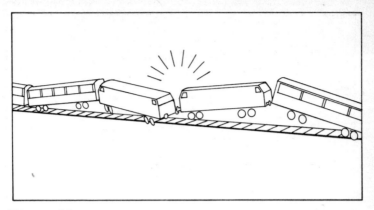

Figure 13

include how you imagined the trains coming into collision (Fig. 13), followed by what you actually found on arrival (Fig. 16).

I call Fig. 12 the 'new starting-point'. It is the point you return to when you rewind this film.

Finally, let the film run along until your memory fades.

THE REWIND

The second film is called the rewind. You don't exactly watch the rewind. You are actually in it, *experiencing* it *in* the screen, seeing everything as if it were happening to you now. The really odd thing is that you will be seeing and feeling everything happening *backwards*.

Suppose you do arrive at the scene of the event to find the two trains that have collided, as in

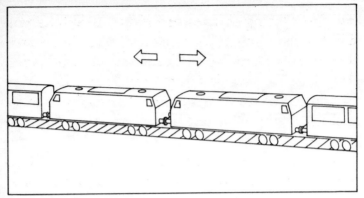

Figure 14

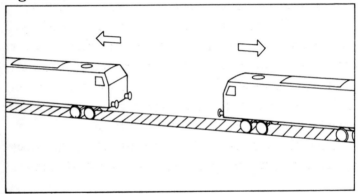

Figure 15

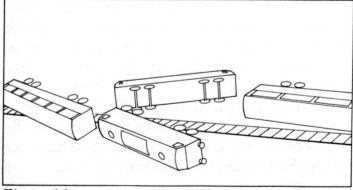

Figure 16

160

Fig. 16. During this rewind phase, in which you will be watching from *inside the screen*, the trains will start pulling apart from one another then travelling backwards away from each other (Figs 14 and 15), until you see them travelling happily and normally as you did at your starting-point (Fig. 12).

Remember, in the rewind you are actually in the film, re-experiencing the event, which is now, however, all happening in reverse.

The rewind must be done rapidly. You may find this difficult at first. If so, practise it slowly to start with. When you've got it right, run it through straight after the forward film.

To give you an idea of the speed of the rewind, if the forward film takes one minute the rewind should take 10–15 seconds at the most.

You should end the rewind at your 'new starting-point', which represents a good image.

To sum up, with the forward film, you are sitting in the centre of the cinema, leaving your body there and floating to the projection room, from where you will watch the forward film. Begin with your new starting-point. Run the first film until it fades.

At this point get into the film. You are no longer watching the film, but re-experiencing the traumatic event in reverse. Rewind the event rapidly. End with your new starting-point.

I must warn you that going through the first film

can be painful and, if a person dear to you is sitting next to you, he or she may well see you becoming pale, sweaty or even tearful. Please don't be put off, either of you. Remember that this should be the last time you will have to remember the event in this way.

After this treatment you will find that, whenever the memory is sparked off, the rewind will rapidly come into play, and will, on its way back, scramble the sequence, leading you very quickly to the new starting-point. The new starting-point is a good image and that is the memory you will be left with. This process will happen faster and faster as every day goes by. As a result of this treatment, you will find that you are now able to resume all the activities you haven't been able to do for a long time.

SOME DIFFICULTIES YOU MAY ENCOUNTER

Some people find rewinding difficult and slow to do at first. Don't be discouraged; practise the rewind on its own until you get it right. Then go through the complete sequence without hesitation or stopping.

Some people often don't have the courage to look at the film in its full detail. It is fairly common to find people wanting to gloss over the really frightening or ugly part. If you do this, you will find that your PTSD symptoms will not disappear completely. You will therefore have to go back and deal with that particular section again, and since this will be particularly unpleasant it makes sense to have someone close to you when you do the rewind.

A NEW MEMORY ARISES

You may be deeply shocked to find that, once you have got rid of a major haunting memory, another one appears. This shouldn't surprise you. Quite often we suppress several disturbing images and, once the major one has been removed, the next most disturbing rises to take its place. If a deeper, concealed memory surfaces, just deal with it in the same way – rewind it.

Don't overreact and think that there may be hundreds more. The greatest number I've treated in one person is four.

THE SECOND IES QUESTIONNAIRE

Fill in your second IES questionnaire two weeks after doing the rewind technique. Compare the result with your first questionnaire to judge how effective the treatment has been in releasing you from the trauma trap.

IES QUESTIONNAIRE

NAME _____

ON _____ YOU EXPERIENCED_____
(DATE)   (LIFE EVENT)

Below is a list of comments made by people after stressful life events. Please check each item, indicating how frequently these comments were true for you DURING THE PAST SEVEN DAYS. If they did not occur during that time, please mark the 'not at all' column.

FREQUENCY

	Not at all	Rarely	Sometimes	Often
1 I thought about it when I didn't mean to.				
2 I avoided letting myself get upset when I thought about it or was reminded of it.				
3 I tried to remove it from my memory.				
4 I had trouble falling asleep or staying asleep, because of pictures or thoughts about it that came into my mind.				
5 I had waves of strong feelings about it.				
6 I had dreams about it.				
7 I stayed away from reminders of it.				
8 I felt as if it hadn't happened or it wasn't real.				
9 I tried not to talk about it.				
10 Pictures about it popped into my mind.				
11 Other things kept making me think about it.				
12 I was aware that I still had a lot of feelings about it, but I didn't deal with them.				
13 I tried not to think about it.				
14 Any reminder brought back feelings about it.				
15 My feelings about it were kind of numb.				

164

8

IN THEIR OWN WORDS

Interviews with Former Sufferers

Before you begin reading this chapter, I should make it clear that I did not personally interview my ex-patients. I wanted to show that these people whom I had successfully treated were well and truly out of the trauma trap and did not need me to reinforce their sense of well-being.

When I asked these people if they were willing to be interviewed, they all generously agreed and all gave the same reason for giving up their time – 'If it will help other people to avoid going through what I went through, then I'm happy to do it.'

The following accounts are given as they were related by my former patients. That is why occasionally an incident is told out of sequence or something is repeated or elaborated on during the course of the interview. The words of the interviewer are printed in italic type.

THE WOMAN WHO NEARLY
DROWNED
Daphne Shaw

Mrs Shaw is now in her mid-fifties, smartly
dressed and quietly spoken. The traumatic event, a
near-drowning which was the cause of her PTSD,
happened some five years ago.

*Had you ever heard of PTSD before you came along
for treatment?*

No, I'd never heard of it. We're all under stress
in our jobs and I suppose I've had the normal
amount of stress in my life. But after this accident
I was confronted with not being able to face seeing
things.

Did you go to your doctor first?

No, I didn't go to see my family doctor. My
husband realized that I was under this terrible
stress and he arranged for me to come here. He
said, 'I think you ought to see someone', and I
agreed. I'll tell you what happened.

It happened in 1986. It was the day before my
birthday in October. We'd been on holiday in
Spain – we have a place in the south of Spain and
we have a sailing boat. I'm not a good sailor but I
crew for my husband. He loves it, but I'm always
nervous. This day, we went out – only in the bay
– and the wind came from both points and just
turned the boat over. I was trapped under the boat

in a little pocket of air and I had a rope round my ankle. I remember thinking, 'I've come up more than three times.' I thought, 'If Roger doesn't save me, I'm going to drown.' He kept diving around and then he caught hold of my foot and he dragged me up.

After that, we did everything wrong. The first rule is, you stay where you are, but we decided to make for the shore – about a mile. We both swim. But then he started to flag. I said, 'Lie on your back and float.' I felt that I could carry on swimming and floating. Then one of the local fishing boats saw what had happened and came out to get us.

We were taken to the local hospital. I looked at my husband and Roger was grey. I thought he was having a heart attack. At the hospital they treated us, then they let us go home in the afternoon. They told us to take it easy, but we'd booked to go out for a meal – for my birthday, I suppose. I can remember sitting in the restaurant and closing my eyes. Roger said, 'You've just relived it all.' My husband is very sensitive to how I feel. I must have gone very quiet and still. I remember closing my eyes and thinking, 'Oh God, what could have happened!'

We finished the holiday as planned and came home. When we got back I found I couldn't watch anything with the sea in it or people in boats – couldn't watch it at all. I saw a film with a big liner going over and I started hyperventilating. Roger realized I was not going to get over this without help, so he rang and made an appointment for me to see the doctor. There was only a few weeks' gap between the incident and seeing the doctor.

The worst things were that I could see Roger literally drowning before my eyes. I'd been in a little pocket of air. I knew I was going to get tired. I knew eventually I was going to die. Once my husband had rescued me I was more worried about him. He'd used a lot of energy trying to get the boat back over. I knew the sea would buoy me up. I knew I could turn over and float. But it was October and the sea was cold.

There was a crowd on the shore when we got there. They'd come to rescue us and they took us in the ambulance to the nearest hospital. I'd had a swimsuit and a sweatshirt top but I went home in a taxi in a hospital gown sellotaped up the back.

Some friends live in the next villa and they've got a set of keys, so Roger went to get them because we'd lost our keys in the boat. He just told them we'd had a spot of bother and ended up in hospital and that I was in the taxi, so they came to our apartment to see me while my husband went to look at the boat. I was quiet – it was an effort to talk to them. I told them about it, I think. I think I cried and got very upset, then Roger came back. I'm one of those who want to go into a corner when I'm in trouble.

That evening, both of us got restless. I said,

'Can we still go out for a meal?' I can't tell you what we ate and neither of us slept much that night. All that Roger could see was me drowning.

When you came along the first time, did you know what the treatment would consist of?

My husband had told me that David had treated people for different traumas, but I couldn't talk about it – it upset me. I couldn't talk about it, so I asked my husband to come with me to the hospital. Roger told David the story of what happened and I started to hyperventilate. Then David asked my husband to leave the room and he made me tell him the story again – to get me over the distress, sort of thing. I did. Then he asked me to go through it backwards. I did. I had to close my eyes and relive it as though watching it in a movie. I could take as long as I liked. Then I had to reverse it and come out of it, which I did.

Could you describe it in more detail?

Well, I was in an armchair, a high-backed chair, and the doctor made me face the wall, as though I was looking at a screen. I had to imagine that the wall was a screen and visualize everything that had happened, from setting foot in the boat to being back in the apartment.

It was just like turning the camera and watching it again, it was so vivid. I'm sure he asked me what was my worst moment and I said, 'My worst moment was being under the boat.' That was awful. It all happened in slow motion. When the boat was turning over, my husband shouted, 'Jump!' I said, 'I can't, I'm caught!' I had this little pocket of air and I was trying to get the rope off my foot. I was struggling to survive – you do, don't you? Suddenly, there was Roger's hand on my ankle. It seemed an eternity, but it was all over in a couple of minutes, I suppose.

Did seeing it on the cinema screen take as long as when it happened in real life?

Doing it in reverse took longer. You have to think harder – remember all the details. David made me go over it. He didn't make me go over it all. The most important part was being under the boat and he made me relive that again.

What happened when you had rewound it? You said, 'OK, I've finished'?

He asked me how I felt and I could answer him quite truthfully. I felt much calmer. He said that if I felt myself getting distressed, I should do the movie forwards and backwards. I still get . . . no, I don't still get upset when I see television pictures of people going into boats and getting off boats, but I *do* still get a bit upset when it shows underwater scenes with people in distress. Now, when I see what happened I see it as it actually happened. I don't have to reverse it any more.

It obviously worked for me, maybe because we caught it in the early stages. That's what I've thought since.

How have you been since that time?

If anybody had said that I would place myself in the same sort of situation again, I wouldn't have believed it. But I did.

It was a real feat for me to go out with my husband in this sailing boat. He was in the Navy and loves sailing. And it is nice – it's so nice to go out in a boat where we are in Spain, the scenery is so nice. Roger is very conscious of how I am and will never push me to my limits. But the daughter-in-law of our neighbours in the next villa is very, very nervous of going in a boat and I was able to help her and that made me feel good. Before the treatment, I couldn't have coped with someone else's stress but after only one session I felt fine.

Now, if I do remember it, it has to be triggered and I can go through it again as I have with you.

I knew I needed help and I'm fully aware of the fact that situations arise where you need help. You've got to face up to things – you've got to help yourself, and the first step towards helping yourself is admitting you need help. Then it becomes easier. A lot of people think they'd lose self-respect because they needed help. I don't see it that way. It's the first step towards healing.

IMAGINATION AND PTSD
Barbara Drake

Mrs Drake, a woman in her late thirties and normally a cheerful person, suffered from PTSD as a result of discovering that her son had been sexually abused by someone in a position of trust. Although the trauma had not happened directly to her, such were the images she had of what her son had gone through that she was unable to control them. Her husband had not suffered from PTSD himself, but was present during our interview.

How soon after the event did you come for treatment?

Mrs Drake: I came two or three times. It's under two years since I first saw Dr Muss.

What happened when you came the first time?

Mrs Drake: He asked me what it was in particular I kept thinking about – any specific thought that kept coming into my mind.
  In some ways it was easier to talk about it. Well, it helps with any problem to talk about it, doesn't it?

Mr Drake: My wife did most of the talking. He asked questions – it made it easier.

Did you both have problems?

Mr Drake: No, I thought I was coping with it. Mind you, I could kill the bloke. No, I didn't try the treatment – it wouldn't work for me – but Dr Muss told me, 'You're coping all right.'

Mrs Drake: We'll tell you what happened. Our son was eleven at the time and a member of a football team. The trainer took the boys away.

Mr Drake: I didn't really want him to go – policemen tend to be overprotective – but then we thought, 'We'll let him go and stay with him.' Later, we found out that the trainer was being charged with serious sexual assault on the boys. They didn't know anything, you see. He'd been drugging them. Our son didn't know anything about it.

Mrs Drake: But the case put our son through a lot. We didn't know whether we should let him go to court.

Mr Drake: I thought that other kids should be protected. When we saw the sentence he got, I regret it. He got nine years – he'll be out in five.

Mrs Drake: Our son didn't know about it, but he was interviewed by the police and examined physically by the police. Some of the other lads, his friends, were too.

We didn't want to talk to anyone else about it.

Mr Drake: We tried a self-help group – it was the latest fashion – but it didn't get us anywhere, just sitting around in a circle listening to other people. In the village where we live it was a five-minute wonder.

Mrs Drake: Justin said, 'Mum, please don't tell anybody.'

Mr Drake: We're still watching him a lot. The younger lad mentioned the man's name. We said, 'Shh.' Justin went quiet. He's very deep.

Mrs Drake: I felt the bottom had fallen out of my world. Well, it is a traumatic experience at half past six on a Monday night to have a policeman turn up on your doorstep. They told us in February, on a Monday, and the court case was in September. It was a long day, Tuesday, at the police station. I kept imagining what had happened.

How did these thoughts come to you?

Mrs Drake: I'd be doing ordinary things then, you know, these images that come into your mind.

I hit the bottle a bit at night. For five or six weeks I was so irritable. I didn't want to know anything. I didn't want to do anything. They mentioned Dr Muss to Harry at the federation and he thought we should try anything to make me feel better.

What happened when you came for treatment?

Mrs Drake: The first time, I told him the story from start to finish. The rewind made a big difference.

Mr Drake: It was very good. She was much better.

Mrs Drake: I came a second time so that he could see how I was. It was the following week. I felt so much better. It was very easy to follow the treatment – I had no problem. That image hadn't come back unless I had consciously thought about it.

Could you tell me about the treatment?

Mrs Drake: I had to stare at a blank wall and see the scene, then rewind. It doesn't bother me now; I'm in control of it.

Had you tried any other form of help before you saw the doctor?

Mrs Drake: I never thought of going to the family doctor. I always thought, 'It's our business, we'll sort it out.'

Mr Drake: You can't always do it on your own. I thought people who sought any kind of help were off their trolley – I now realize they're not.

Mrs Drake: Until you've tried it, don't knock it.

Mr Drake: The big thing is that my good lady's all right, so I'm all right.

What reaction did the rest of the family have?

Mrs Drake: The older girl, now seventeen, got upset first off. The younger lad sensed something was not quite right. He's only eight. Actually, it's one of the few times they've hit it off. They've been closer since then. We all have.

A DELAYED CASE OF PTSD
Martin Brody

This young man, then in his early thirties, was one of the West Midlands police who were sent to Liverpool to interview people involved with the Hillsborough disaster – both the survivors and the families of those who were killed. Some time after his return from the investigation the reaction set in.

How did you come to hear about the treatment?

I realized that I'd got some sort of problem and called my own doctor out. He offered me some tablets and gave me the address of a local psychiatrist. My brother suggested getting in touch with the Police Benevolent Department and the guy there identified the problem straight away and recommended I see Dr Muss. I didn't want anyone else to know what was going on and so it seemed ideal to be seen out of my normal environment.

What sort of state were you in when you went for treatment?

I couldn't handle anything. I would battle through work for eight hours, thinking sleep would make it all right the next day. Sometimes my mind was racing at a million miles an hour. Sleep was no problem, though I'd wake up occasionally.

I turned to the demon drink. I would try to knock myself out. I would look at other people and think, 'If only you knew what I'm going through!' I had this feeling of loneliness. I was irritable, edgy, jumpy. I'd snap at people. I don't suffer fools gladly. It made decision making very difficult.

After the Hillsborough investigation I came back on a Thursday and went back into my normal routine on the Monday. The only contact we had was a letter from the Assistant Chief Constable – just a pro forma letter. We also had one large debrief to thank us and sort out administrative problems. There was no follow-up. The only offer we had while we were up there was from two people from the Welfare Department, who said, 'We're here if you've got problems.' It wasn't until eight months after I got back that it started and then it developed very quickly.

I feel that it's a big stigma throughout the force: you're some kind of outcast. I told no one at work. One colleague at work knows, but I've been very wary in letting people know. The trouble with our job is that you can't be seen to be weak. I've heard that another in the group also suffered, but I don't know who.

There were 400 police officers altogether. The Lord Chief Justice wanted the West Midlands Force to investigate it up in Liverpool and we worked with the families of people who went to the match. There were 150 of us at Liverpool.

Had you been around when the disaster happened at Hillsborough?

I was working the afternoon it happened. Then I was in my parents' house and I couldn't work out what was going on. I didn't see the papers and I'd sort of forgotten about it – it didn't crop up.

In Liverpool I was talking to the families and other police officers and other civilian people who'd gone to the match – I saw perhaps a hundred people, all of whom knew someone who'd died at the game. You get so used to dealing with people who've lost relations. You've got to sit some of them down and in some cases it could take eight or nine hours to get the information from them. Some of the police were trying to do a little bit of counselling themselves. Some people went over the top, but at the time it was just one of those things. We were paid overtime to do it and living in a four-star hotel. No problems. I saw all the videos – they didn't really bother me.

One incident upset me. It was a recurring factor in the problems I had later.

In December we had a family problem and I couldn't handle it before Christmas. Then after Christmas I received a complaint from a man who accused me of wrongful arrest. This hit me. I was in a dreadful state over it. I didn't know why I couldn't handle it in the same way as I'd handled the rest.

Then on the Thursday I was driving a police car and had an accident. It was really my fault. Afterwards I was due to play in a football match and I felt very wound up. I thought the game would get it out, but I cried all the way home.

I didn't realize it was Hillsborough. I seemed to deteriorate very quickly. I saw Dr Muss in the next few days. At the first session we just talked. He said, 'I don't want to know your problems – they might upset me.' He seemed to grasp what I was saying. He said, 'No problem. We can cure it.' I felt, 'Great! I'm on my way back.' It was unbelievable. I explained about the flashbacks. I went three times. I had a minor relapse and went back and he treated me in much the same way. Since then I've never felt better.

When he asked you to see the scene up on the screen, did you have any difficulty?

No. It's not at all hard to picture yourself. I felt a bit of a fool. I thought, 'This isn't going to work.' But Dr Muss is very easy to speak to and I relaxed very quickly.

I got very upset when I pictured myself. I became very upset at the images but I got them out. I've been working on them myself between sessions.

Had you tried any other form of help before you came for the treatment?

I tried my own way but my own doctor couldn't help me. I hate to think of the sort of state I would have been in. Perhaps I wouldn't have got back. That's one of my great worries – I don't want to get like [a colleague].

How long did you think it would take?

I thought it would last months and months. I couldn't believe how quick it was – so quick and simple. I was off work for a month then I went back to work.

Later, there was a problem at home and on the second occasion I had no time off work. When I realized something was wrong I went back to see Dr Muss. I could feel my mind going again. I saw him twice and I was back on the tracks. This was exactly a year ago. Thinking about it, the difference between the way I am now and the way I was twelve months ago is a million miles.

Has anything positive come out of this experience?

Yes. I remember being frightened; I thought I was going insane. I couldn't see myself getting back to my normal self. Now I've changed for the better. I'm a more sensitive person. I can express my emotional feelings better, more easily. I can cry. I've learned to be far more open – I can feel other people's emotions. Maybe because of my work I'd become hard. I'm far more patient.

Since all this, I've transferred to CID duties and I'm enjoying life as well as I ever did. I think I could go and deal with it – be on an inquiry team – if I had to. There have been incidents at work in the past twelve months and I just go straight into the technique. If I can feel it coming on I just go off and sit in the toilet and after ten minutes I'm fine.

I'll tell you what the images were. I was fourteen weeks away from home, staying in a four-star hotel and working twelve hours a day. I was with my mates and having a good time. In our time off, we'd be visiting places and I enjoyed myself. I felt satisfied in the work I'd done.

The flashbacks had to do with when I went to see a senior officer. He'd been in the force for a long time and he was in pieces. You could see it in his face.

I went with another lad (we worked in pairs) and knocked on the door. A girl answered and I asked for the officer. She showed me the house. Her fiancé had been killed. We went to the right house and saw our police officer. I sat on the settee and had a can of beer. I could see it in his face – it was ashen. You wouldn't think it. You'd imagine he'd seen everything.

He has a son and his son's friend from school often used to come and sit on the settee and wait for them. He used to sit on the seat I was sitting on – on that side of the settee. The worst image was that man's face and myself sitting on the settee where this poor lad used to sit.

Since November I've no longer been able to see the man's face, though I try. Now I can talk about any aspect of it. I'm in control.

THE MAN WHO BELIEVED HE WAS GOING TO BE SHOT
Guy Proctor

A man in his thirties with two young children, Guy Proctor was on duty as a policeman when he was attacked by three men, one of whom turned a shotgun on him. Although he was not badly hurt physically, he had been in fear of his life and he got into a desperate condition before he sought help for his PTSD.

When did all this take place?

I consulted Dr Muss in March 1988. I was a police officer at the time, driving a panda on my own. I saw this chap trying to steal a car and when he saw me he jumped into a van and drove off. I followed him, but it turned out that the van had three men in it and they'd been trying to swap getaway cars. It got as far as Handsworth and then they blocked the road in front of me. Before I could get out they came up to the car and started attacking it and threatened my life. I was looking down a shotgun barrel. They didn't shoot me. Physically, all I had was a few bumps and bruises, but I thought I was dead.

I had five days at home then I went back to work. Within the first few days I was getting very severe headaches. I was driving the same repaired vehicle on the same beat. I went to my doctor and he said it was psychosomatic, caused by severe tension. I went off sick for a further ten days.

When I was at work, every time the radio went I was dreading it being for me. I was panicky. When I was in the same area, I'd mentally blank it out. I was so tense that it felt as though someone had cut the back of my head off. The headaches were getting worse. The doctor said to take some time off. He gave me some tablets to calm me down – betablockers. They helped a little bit but the most help was being away from policing.

The incident was all over the papers and in the evening news on the TV. It was traumatic for me and the family, but it didn't put me off policing. A lot of police are afraid to go and see a psychiatrist even if they have a desperate need.

What happened when you went to see Dr Muss?

I told him the story. I had a very, very clear recollection of all the events. The problem with police work was that if anyone mentioned a word or phrase it would immediately get me tensed up again. Anything, any trigger would set me off again. I couldn't get away from it. A report about a stolen motor vehicle, 'running away' – these are everyday phrases in police work.

I went on my own and went through it in detail. I had to imagine sitting in a cinema watching an incident performed by an actor. Then I had to fast reverse the whole sequence of events. I had to run through as quickly as I could to the beginning. He said, 'You should be finishing about now.' I hadn't

183

quite finished. I did that two or three times the first session. I thought it was a bit daft. I was expecting something different and I thought, 'I don't need to go there!' I was off work, helping in a garden centre and still suffering from the headaches – always uptight and tense.

Then I was back at work and getting the headaches again. I had another session with Dr Muss and it was much the same thing as before – talking it through. I'd put in a claim for criminal injuries compensation and needed a report from Dr Muss. To analyse the treatment, I went to a second session. It was amazing. I thought he'd do something to take away the memory, but I can remember everything as clear as today. It doesn't bother me. I can pick it up at any point in the sequence of events. It probably lasted fifteen minutes. I know now it's gone, it's past. It doesn't jump into my mind when I don't want it to. It used to jump up and hit me in the face.

It took me some months to get over it properly, but I couldn't get away from it before I saw Dr Muss. Afterwards, it was not affecting me in the same way. There's a lot of adrenalin in police work. You can get irritable and uptight. Now, I'm much more relaxed. I just wish that other people knew that they don't have to suffer. If it helps just one person, I'm glad to have talked to you.

9

OUT OF THE TRAP

Once you have rid yourself of the recurring intrusive images that have marred your life, you are free from the trap. Then, you were running in circles, unable to escape the memories of the trauma; now, you can feel proud that you have regained your former strength and resourcefulness and are able to take on whatever you need to. You may well feel that life is suddenly more wonderful than ever before – being relieved of an intolerable burden can have that effect. A few of you may still need to cope with other difficulties brought on by your illness and the circumstances which brought it about. The great thing is that you are now in a position to deal with any other problems you may have.

These could include a number of physical ailments, as well as alcoholism, depression, apathy and drug abuse. These were overlaid by the intense pain of being unable to prevent yourself from reliving the trauma which was at the root of your PTSD, but now that you are free from that you must look to the rest of your worries and try to eliminate them. In other words, you must take steps to get yourself back to health, both mental and physical. You will find that your renewed confidence in yourself will give you strength, and those around you – family, friends, colleagues at work and neighbours – will be delighted to see you preparing to tackle these difficulties.

ALCOHOLISM

The pain and stress of PTSD pushes some people into alcohol abuse. If you are one of those, you will be feeling stronger now and able to take action to get your life back on an even keel. What route you take is up to you, but I suggest that you see your family doctor, or contact an organization such as Alcoholics Anonymous, or both. It is also very important that you tell the people close to you that you are determined to give up your dependence on drink. It will be very reassuring for them and it means that they will give you their support at a time when you will certainly need it.

How resorting to the bottle can conceal deeper problems is illustrated by the case of Frank Fielding.

This police officer came for treatment in February 1989. He had had a complicated medical history, involving two episodes in which he had collapsed. Following the second of these, tests on his liver indicated that there was an alcohol problem. This was masking the underlying stress which had brought on PTSD. Mr Fielding was advised to give up drinking alcohol and did so for a while, and a couple of months later he was back at work.

Despite his problems, Mr Fielding's work had not suffered. He continued to be commended but he was just not relaxing and when he got home at night he took to taking a couple of glasses of wine with his meals. Unfortunately, as the stress got greater, the couple of glasses turned into a couple of bottles. On one occasion he drank three bottles of wine in one day and became verbally abusive.

The family went on holiday the following year and things came to a head. The holiday was, in his own words, a disaster – because he couldn't switch off. In the September after the holiday there was another weekend when he got through three bottles of wine. Matters continued to deteriorate until December, when he went to see his doctor, who prescribed Librium.

On that occasion Mr Fielding promised his wife that if he had another weekend as bad as that one he would get himself right. Not long after, early in the new year, he drank four bottles of wine and a doctor was called out to see him. He complained of awful nightmares, but the doctor was inclined to see him as an alcoholic. Mr Fielding denied that this was so, but the doctor (not his regular one) advised him to stay at home for a month.

Mr Fielding went in to work as normal because he had a strong sense of responsibility to his colleagues. At his particular station, he felt, they were overwhelmed with work and he admitted that he never refused a request to do something and also that he was bad at delegating – he tried to do everything himself. 'I worry a lot and I never turn anyone down. I allow other people to tell me their problems, but I keep mine to myself.'

Although his colleagues continued to find him satisfactory at work, his private life was in bad shape. He felt socially inadequate, whereas once he had been happy-go-lucky. He also complained that he felt unable to give to his family and found concentration difficult – he even found it hard to read a newspaper.

It emerged that he had been having nightmares every night for over a year. Alcohol was his only solace. The recurring nightmare concerned an old lady who had hanged herself. He had been called to the scene of the suicide before his first collapse in 1985 and, although he had seen some terrible sights in his career, this hit him hard because he knew the lady concerned. The image of this old lady, who powerfully reminded him of his grandmother, had stayed with him ever since. Another nightmare he frequently had involved him being knocked to the ground and unable to get up because he was too heavy.

Once he was relaxed, Mr Fielding tried the

rewind technique on the actual event he saw in his nightmare and reported feeling very much better straight away. Ten days later he came for another consultation and said that he couldn't believe what had happened. He had slept very well and had had no nightmares since. His wife said that he had been much more relaxed and they had been out quite a lot.

Mr Fielding came for one final consultation a week later and was delighted. He was feeling great – more interested in everything and able to go back to work.

DEPRESSION

The fact that you are reading this book confirms, in a way, that you have fortunately not become clinically depressed.

Many PTSD sufferers can be tormented for so long that in the end they exhaust their mental reserves and become so low that they no longer want to try to help themselves. They have lost all confidence and belief in themselves and in the professionals.

You may have friends or relations who are exactly like this. You may well feel frustrated that they are refusing to read this book to help themselves. The only way to resolve the problem is by getting them out of the depressed state. Depression is such a common problem that most GPs are able to offer effective drug treatment which will lift the person out of the depression within two months.

As soon as the depression dissolves, you will find that the person becomes receptive and enthusiastic again. However, as the haunting memories will still be there, the benefit will not last unless these memories can be wiped out. This, then, is the time to try out the rewind technique. Your friend or relative will now be willing and able to go through with it, and will finally get out of the trap.

ORGANIZATIONS WHICH CAN HELP

The organizations listed below can offer counselling and practical help in dealing with personal problems. Elsewhere in this chapter we will look at how to deal with problems that concern the outside world – claiming compensation and suing for damages.

Terrence Higgins Trust (AIDS)	071-843 2971
Alcoholics Anonymous	0904-644026
Alcoholics Anonymous (Australia)	02-799 1199
ACCEPT (Drinkwatchers)	071-381 3155
CRUSE (bereavement)	081-940 4818
Compassionate Friends (bereaved parents)	0272-292778

Cot Death Research and Support for Bereaved Parents	0836-219010
Gay Bereavement Project	081-455 8894
Disfigurement Guidance Centre	0334-55746
Incest Crisis Line	081-422 5100
Incest Survivors Association (Australia)	09-227 8745
London Rape Crisis Centre	071-837 1600
Survivors (sexual abuse of men)	071-833 8116
British Association for Counselling	0788-578328
Westminster Pastoral Foundation	071-937 6956
Asian Family Counselling Service	
London	081-997 5749
Bradford	0274-720 486
Samaritans	0753-32713
Depressives Anonymous	0482-860619
MIND (mental problems)	071-637 0741
Turning Point (drugs)	071-606 3947
Release (drugs)	071-377 5905
Drug Research and Rehabilitation (Australia)	09-321 3191
Association of Drug Referral Centres (Australia)	02-977 2197
Gamblers Anonymous	071-352 3060
Nexus (loneliness)	081-367 6328
Outsiders Club (disablement/loneliness)	071-499 0900
Relate (relationships)	0788-573241
Scottish Marriage Guidance Council	031-225 5006

Catholic Marriage Advisory Council	071-371 1341
Jewish Marriage Guidance Council	071-203 6311
Organization for Parents Under Stress	0268-757077
Parents of Murdered Children Support Group	0702-68510
Salvation Army	071-236 5222
BACUP (cancer)	071-608 1661
Cancer Information and Support Society (Australia)	02-817 1912
ASH (Action on Smoking and Health)	071-637 9843
Marylebone Centre Trust (stress)	071-487 7415
Positive Health Centre (stress)	071-935 1811
Yoga for Health Foundation (stress)	0767-27271
Victim Support	071-735 9166
Victim Support Scotland	031-558 1380
Irish Association for Victim Support	0001-798673

COMPENSATION

It may be that, now your main problem of PTSD has been resolved by the treatment, you don't need the kind of help described above. You may be able to resolve any remaining difficulties in your own life and feel that you want to state your case in society. If this is so, you will wish to know how to claim for compensation or how to go about suing for damages.

The first thing to say about compensation is that it fulfils two very important functions. First, it provides financial help for people who may desperately need it, thereby relieving some of the additional strain brought on by anxieties about money. Second, it is a formal and public recognition of the suffering the victim and the victim's family have had to endure.

Speaking about claims for injury caused by criminal acts, the Director of Victim Support, Helen Reeves, believes that 'Compensation is an important way of acknowledging that . . . crime is not acceptable. The gesture is as important as the value of the money involved.'

In the United Kingdom, the legal position is evolving even now. There is no doubt that PTSD is accepted by the law as a legitimate head of damages but ignorance of the condition is still widespread and there is still a sense that an intangible injury is less disabling than something visible, like the loss of a limb.

The actual sum awarded is often badly needed, for many victims of PTSD are unable to go on working. The long delays of the legal procedure make the situation critical for many people who have been scraping by, waiting for the case to come before an arbitrator. In some cases, they build up debts in expectation of the award they feel they are due, and if that is not granted the outlook for them is very bleak.

There is also a very important need for recognition, which is satisfied by having one's case upheld by an independent judge. After a trauma which has disrupted one's life, it is necessary for most people to let the world know what they have gone through. It gives them a sense that they have resumed control of their lives.

COMPENSATION AFTER AN ACCIDENT

If you have been involved in an accident, you may wish to check if you are entitled to compensation. In England, you can go to a law firm which displays a sign of a bandaged thumb in its window and ask for a free interview. Someone there will advise you whether you can claim compensation and, if you seem to have a case, they will proceed from there.

If you are claiming for psychiatric injury, you will need to have an independent assessment carried out by a psychiatrist or a psychologist, and your solicitor can recommend one. Most people worry that this will involve them in huge expense, but this is seldom the case. The solicitor usually pays for the report and recovers the fee from the insurance company concerned, whereas if you qualify for legal aid the cost will be reimbursed by the scheme.

Cases where victims have sued for damages after being caught up in disasters are considered later. Two examples are the survivors of the *Herald of Free Enterprise*, the ferry which went down at Zeebrugge with the loss of 187 lives, who received awards for a variety of injuries, some of whom cited PTSD; and a booking clerk who recently received damages on account of the PTSD he suffered following the King's Cross fire.

COMPENSATION AFTER CRIMINAL INJURY

Few people feel at ease with legal and medical formalities at the best of times and much less so when they are suffering from the after-effects of trauma, but the law exists to see justice done and you may well be entitled to claim compensation if you have been the victim of a crime.

The body concerned with such matters in Great Britain is the Criminal Injuries Compensation Board, the CICB. In order to qualify for compensation, the victim of the crime must have suffered personal injury, including shock, which is 'directly attributable to a crime of violence or to a threat of violence' and, generally speaking, the person who inflicted the injury must have been prosecuted unless there are good reasons why not.

The rules also stipulate that the injury must be serious enough to warrant a compensation payment of at least £550. The board makes the kind of award that a court would make for similar injuries.

The CICB does not grant compensation to victims of traffic accidents in the ordinary way. It states: 'Although certain traffic offences are crimes of violence (for example, motor manslaughter and furious driving or reckless driving or cycling) they are also traffic offences. An application based on an injury arising from these offences will be considered by the Board only if compensation is not available to the victim under motor vehicle or cycle insurance.'

In other words, most cases of injury by motor vehicle will be covered by an insurance policy and it is against the insurers that the victim should claim.

The rules governing what is or is not admissible can best be explained to you by someone who is familiar with the procedure and it might be advisable for you to get in touch with the Law Society (071-242 1222) or your local Citizens' Advice Bureau to see if you qualify for legal aid or some other scheme to assist you.

It is only fair to tell you at this stage that between 1989 and 1990 the CICB received 53,655 new applications for compensation and that 80 per cent of all cases took over twelve months to settle. Do not expect your application to be dealt with straight away. Nevertheless, during that year the board did make 38,620 awards, which was 39 per cent up on the previous year.

Victim Support gave evidence to the House of

Commons Select Committee on Home Affairs when it was conducting an enquiry into the way the CICB operates. The committee found evidence of a 'scandalous backlog' of compensation applications and recommended the appointment of sixty extra staff, something which the government accepted. The report stated that the aim of compensation in these cases is 'to alleviate the suffering and shock experienced by victims of violent crime and to demonstrate society's concern for them'.

The CICB can be contacted on 041-221 0495 and a guide to the scheme, a leaflet called 'Victims of Crimes of Violence', is issued by Her Majesty's Stationery Office.

A BACKGROUND TO COMPENSATION

The whole concept of compensation is relatively new. In the past, when there was a terrible fire or earthquake, it was a natural disaster, an act of God, and no one could be held responsible. But eventually it was recognized that where a catastrophe had occurred as the result of someone else's negligence there was a case to be made for the victim's right to sue for compensation.

In the early days, the grounds on which you could sue were fairly primitive. If you lost a leg or had your spine broken, the damage was self-evident, and the suffering you experienced was included in with the physical injury. The idea of psychological damage did not begin to gain ground until after the First World War. The appalling conditions in the trenches and the type of warfare where nerves were stretched to snapping point led doctors and psychiatrists to look into what was known at the time as shell shock. A great number of soldiers who had been decorated for gallantry went on to suffer from shell shock, among them the poet Siegfried Sassoon, but this did not stop the army from shooting some of them for cowardice or desertion.

Freud became interested, and developed his theory that life is a struggle and our desire to be free from tension leads to a death wish. Millais tried to get those suffering from shell shock to talk though their experiences as a way of bringing the deep-seated memories and fears to the surface, and people in society at large came to realize that ordinary men and women could suffer from illnesses seated in the mind without them being 'mad'.

After the Second World War the world became aware of the terrible calamity the bombing of Hiroshima and Nagasaki had been for the people involved. Survivors suffered from massive anxiety and depression and many had the feeling that life was not worth living. Survivors of the concentration camps had similar attitudes, as did many prisoners of war held by the Japanese and the Nazis. That war had left very deep scars on millions of people. But after that time, the idea was accepted that the human mind cannot withstand certain unbearable pressures and that ordinary people who had been obliged to live through an extraordinary experience might require psychological intervention to help them back to health.

NEW ZEALAND

This country deserves a special mention because it has been quite advanced in its care for the victims of both accidents and crime. In 1982 its Accident Compensation Act treated victims of crime and victims of accident alike in meeting medical expenses and in providing earnings-related benefits. Its Criminal Justice Act (1985) improved procedures for awarding monetary reparation to victims and the Rape Law Reform Act in the same year made court procedures less intimidating for sexual assault victims. The Victims of Offences Act in 1987 required judges to be given impact reports on victims at the time of sentencing offenders and the New Zealand Minister of Justice established a Victims Task Force to help develop suitable services for victims of crime.

BUFFALO CREEK

In the United States in 1972 there was a disaster at a place called Buffalo Creek, a mining town in West Virginia. A dam gave way and a tidal wave of mud swept down the valley, killing 125 people and leaving over 600 injured. Of those survivors, over 90 per cent were seen to be suffering psychologically and 654 people decided to sue the mining company, not just for physical injury but also for psychological stress.

In the end, the court accepted the evidence presented by the plaintiffs and made awards of between $7,500 and $10,000 for psychological distress suffered as a result of the disaster. This created a precedent.

COMPENSATION IN THE UNITED KINGDOM

THE PIPER ALPHA OIL RIG DISASTER

In the United Kingdom lawyers are breaking new ground. After the Piper Alpha oil rig fire, survivors and bereaved families felt heartened by the announcement of Armand Hammer, then chairman of Occidental, that all Occidental workers would receive £100,000. Their relief dissolved, however, when they realized that most of the men working on the rig had been contracted, not directly employed, and were therefore not covered by Occidental's insurance. The majority of the survivors and the families of those who died have had to make claims, some of which are still being settled.

After Occidental made the offer of £100,000 to the families of those who had been directly employed, the natural reaction of most people was to accept and avoid having to get involved in upsetting litigation. Scottish lawyers, however, urged them not to settle, because the company would certainly have had to pay out larger sums in the United States and were getting off lightly. In fact, many families just could not face the long-drawn-out process and were prepared to settle for less if that meant the whole thing would be over quicker.

The group of people who were most badly affected were those who were dependent on those men who had been killed, but whose status in the eyes of the law was not recognized. These included girlfriends and partners who were not legally married. The oil companies were not keen to pay out compensation unless the claimant had a cast-iron right.

In a forthright speech made to the Institute of Petroleum in 1988, Basil Butler, chairman of British Petroleum, made the attitude of the multi-national companies clear. He told the assembly: 'Everything has an economic cost. We have to draw a balance between our expenditure and the levels of safety we achieve. It is as simple and as complex as that.'

MULTI-PARTY SUITS

Following the Bradford City fire disaster, the Law Society set up a committee to co-ordinate the affairs of the various people who were all pursuing the same aims – people involved in a multi-party suit – and this has gone some way towards simplifying what can be a bewildering and painful process.

Damages can be claimed where there is injury and also the claimant can calculate his or her loss of earnings. Naturally enough, the stakes are high for all the parties concerned when the grounds on which someone can claim compensation or sue for damages are extended. The fact that PTSD is now officially recognized as a clinically verifiable disorder and is accepted as a head of compensation has implications for all sorts of bodies, including insurance and assurance companies.

The survivors of the Bradford City fire disaster did not succeed in persuading the courts to award damages on the grounds of psychological damage, but the victims of the Zeebrugge ferry capsize argued their case fiercely and it went to arbitration.

THE P&O *HERALD OF FREE ENTERPRISE*

The ten survivors who determined to take the matter to arbitration instructed the solicitors Pannone Napier, known for their interest in cases involving PTSD, and the arbitrators were three Queen's Counsel (QCs). In their decision, these QCs stated: 'Many of the Zeebrugge victims undoubtedly suffered from PTSD; of course, some victims suffered from some other psychiatric illness, for example depression, at the same time.

'An injury to a limb leaves it vulnerable. It is the same with psychiatric problems. All the claimants will be at risk of further illness in the face of stress which would have affected them less but for their Zeebrugge experience.'

All ten claimants were granted awards for psychiatric injuries, ranging from £1,750 to £30,000. In the latter case, the fifty-four-year-old man who received this, the highest payment, was found to be suffering from a depressive illness, pathological grief and severe PTSD. When one considers that the impact of the disaster on this man's life has been 'catastrophic', this is not a huge sum.

THE KING'S CROSS FIRE

After the fire at King's Cross, London Transport offered most survivors and the families of those who had been killed in the disaster an immediate payment of £2,500. Because the process of the law is often so slow, some of the cases are still being heard at the time of going to press, but I can report that in February 1991 a booking clerk who witnessed the fire and who had retired from work on the grounds of his suffering from PTSD received an award of £50,000. Three months earlier, in December 1990, four firemen who suffered psychological injury in the aftermath of the fire received a total of £34,000 agreed damages in the High Court against London Underground.

THE INDIVIDUAL DISASTER

People tend to forget that most cases of PTSD are brought on not by a single disaster which affects scores or hundreds of people, but by the many disasters of smaller scale which each affect only a few. In May 1990, Birmingham High Court heard a case about a train driver whose diesel was hit head–on by another locomotive. The driver had taken early retirement as a result of the trauma. He told the court, 'The crash has ruined my life. Money does not make up for what I have gone through. I should have been dead. It was only my quick reactions which saved me.'

The court was told by a psychiatrist that the claimant was suffering from PTSD and went on to award him £35,413 in damages.

In 1988 a cashier in a hospital wages department was robbed on two separate occasions. Despite the fact that she had sustained no physical injury, PTSD was diagnosed. She was admitted to hospital, but her range of symptoms – including depression, anxiety and sexual dysfunction – were not relieved and the prognosis for the future was poor. The CICB awarded her £35,000 for psychiatric damage.

THOMAS SHARPLES

This is a story of a patient whose treatment has not yet been completed, but it is an opportunity to see the way a case develops. The background to the case was established at a couple of meetings, then a report was sent to his solicitors.

Mr Sharples was driving his heavy goods vehicle when he had a collision with a motor car which had been speeding. Since the accident, some seven and a half months previously, he had suffered in a number of ways and had finally decided to seek help.

During the first consultation, he talked about the accident, which had happened on a rainy day. He had been on a bend in his lorry when a car came at him at great speed. He tried to brake, and did so, but the other vehicle was going at such speed that it crashed into him with great force and the passenger was killed.

Immediately after the incident, he couldn't

believe what had happened. He got out of his cab and tried to help but couldn't see anyone because of the state of the car, which was smashed to pieces. The next day he went to work as usual and emptied a few skips but felt so bad that he took the lorry back and went home. He managed to sleep, but had to take whisky to help him get off. In the past, he used to have a glass or two, but some nights now he can sink half a bottle. 'I can't settle. I keep thinking about the accident.'

REPORT

TWO WEEKS AFTER THE ACCIDENT
After being off work for two weeks, Mr Sharples resumed driving but found that he could not face driving past the site of the accident and therefore went on 'an absolute detour'. Even so, driving had become a nightmare. This is still the case to date.

SIX WEEKS LATER
Eventually, Mr Sharples decided that he had to try to drive past the place where the accident happened because this was very near his workplace. Though he has managed to do this, his mental state when driving his lorry is one of increased arousal, particularly on a rainy day or if there are 'silly drivers' about.

PRESENT CONDITION
Six months ago Mr Sharples started looking for another job which didn't involve driving, but his prospects in the current economic situation do

not look good. Having to drive a lorry every day acts as a constant reminder of the event, which in turn has had a deleterious effect on his personality. Mr Sharples was described to me by his wife, who accompanied him, as a man who loved his driving – it was his priority in life – and he had an outgoing personality. Since the event, he has become withdrawn, almost a stranger. He is extremely tense when driving with his wife in their own car and the alcohol consumption represents a real worry for Mrs Sharples. Mr Sharples would happily not go to work if he did not need to make a living.

CONCLUSION
Mr Sharples appears on examination to be a very sad, shattered man suffering from severe post-traumatic stress disorder (PTSD). He believes he will never get rid of the images of the accident.

10

AT WORK AND AT HOME

Post-traumatic stress disorder – the trauma trap –
affects the world outside the interior world of the
sufferer. Its implications reach into the workplace
and also affect the family relationships of the
sufferer within the home.

PTSD AND THE WORKPLACE

When someone wanted time off work to visit the
dentist, his boss asked him why he couldn't go in
his own time, not company time. 'Why should I?'
was the reply. 'My teeth rot in company time.'
There is a grain of truth in that old chestnut. We
spend a great part of our days working, and those
who work outside the home may spend longer

out of it, both at work and travelling to and from work, than anywhere else.

It stands to reason, therefore, that statistically we are at least as likely to experience a traumatic event at work as in the home. The trauma may or may not be related to what we do to earn a living, but the fact that it happens in the workplace should be enough to make employers sit up and take notice.

SOME FIGURES

Injuries in the workplace, including fatal injuries, are significant factors in the equation. In the United States, the total number of disabling injuries sustained at work in 1988–9 was 1,800,000. One million eight hundred thousand people injured seriously enough to be either permanently or temporarily disabled. One million eight hundred thousand families caught up in a potential family disaster. The number of deaths in the workplace was 10,600.

In the United Kingdom in the same year there were 2.4 deaths for every hundred thousand people working – 730 people killed – and 19,944 major injuries per 100,000 employees.

WORKING DAYS LOST

We are always reading about how many working days are lost as a result of back pain or the common cold, but it would be a fair bet that many, many days are lost as a result of PTSD. Indeed, some people give up their jobs because they can no longer function normally and some have to look for another way of making a living because their former job reminds them too much of the trauma. Thomas Sharples, the lorry driver mentioned in the previous chapter, had to give up driving a lorry for it just reinforced all the terrible memories he had of the accident which caused his illness.

Quite apart from our natural feeling of compassion for all the ruined lives, for the sick and unhappy people who are not able to make a full contribution to society, this gives us another reason to join in the fight against PTSD. Not only would the world be a happier one if this scourge were eradicated, PTSD is an expensive waste of manpower and resources. We should be campaigning to make employers aware of what they can do to help and that it is in their own interests to do so.

In many cases, it is the very nature of someone's job which puts him or her into a position where they can be subjected to the trauma in the first place. In a few jobs, people are paid danger money but the fact is that a great many jobs carry a risk which is not acknowledged.

CRIME AT WORK

The 1988 *British Crime Survey* estimated that one-quarter of violent offences experienced by working people occur at the workplace. That does not include the offences committed against people on their way to or from their jobs. Those who work unsocial hours are often obliged to travel on public transport in the early hours of the morning or find themselves walking home late at night when few people are about. Employers generally consider that what happens to their employees once they are off the premises is none of their business, but the risks are run as a direct result of the jobs people do.

THE TRAUMA SPECIALIST

In the United States, many offices and factories have a full-time counsellor on the staff and are equipped to deal with a crisis which develops at work or which affects the company's employees. Something along similar lines is what other countries should be considering, because in the medium and long term it will save the company money and will make for a happier and healthier society.

Setting up a centre or making provision for dealing with trauma may entail some costs initially, which is the argument most employers

211

give for failing to implement any improvement in the workplace, but this is a very short-term view of the problem. Not only will they gain by holding on to a healthy workforce with low rates of absenteeism, but they will also avoid the likelihood of being sued for damages.

A DISASTER AT WORK

When the Piper Alpha oil rig disaster took place, the position was different from most previous disasters, because it happened when the men were working. When there is a major train crash or a fire in a public place, most people are there as private citizens, but in this tragedy the men had no choice but to be there because they were working for the company or one of its subcontractors.

Many survivors felt that they could not contemplate returning to work on the rigs. The families of survivors were against it, too, and for some time it became difficult to recruit workers for jobs on the North Sea.

The situation was similar with the workers on the *Herald of Free Enterprise*. Most of the seamen who had been working for P&O left their jobs within the year and abandoned life at sea altogether. Perhaps if a rapid and sensitive response on the part of the employer encouraged workers to explore their problems within the company they would not be obliged to quit their jobs and look elsewhere for employment.

THE SAN DIEGO EXPERIENCES

Let us see how the system operates in the United States. In 1978, a PSA jet and a private Cessna collided over San Diego, killing all 137 passengers and crew and killing a further nine people on the ground. Police and rescue workers had to spend hours searching the area for debris and collecting human remains, which had been scattered as a result of the explosion.

After completing this grisly task, nearly a dozen officers applied for and won stress disability retirements. They had been offered no programme after the trauma to relieve their stress and deal with any signs of the onset of PTSD.

Six years later, in 1984, there was a shooting at a McDonalds, also in San Diego, in which twenty-one adults and children were killed. The very day of the incident, a comprehensive trauma programme was offered to the officers who were involved and on this occasion *no* officers retired as a result of stress.

THE THREE STAGES OF RESPONSE TO TRAUMA

1   THE IMPACT

This can last from hours to days. This is character-ized by shock, numbness, confusion, heightened feelings of vulnerability, helplessness, dependency and fear and anger. Quite commonly, appetite changes are noticed, people have trouble with sleeping and usually avoid at all costs anything which reminds them of the original incident.

2   THE RECOIL

Once the immediate shock is over, victims still have a powerful feeling that the world is no longer a safe place. They wonder if they will ever feel the same again and some may have strong desires for revenge. These emotions, anger and revenge, may be upsetting for people who consider themselves mild, rational and charitable by nature. It is a characteristic of this phase that the victim will endlessly rehearse the incident in his or her own mind and want to talk about it to others.

During this phase, there may be periods when the victim claims not to be thinking about the trauma. These are just resting periods, in order to give the victim time to work out how to get back to normal.

3 REORGANIZATION

This is when feelings are coming under control and the person is beginning to recover his or her former capacity to concentrate and work as effectively as before. This can then resolve itself in a number of ways. Either the person feels more resilient and stronger as a result of the experience or continues to be oversensitive and reacts badly to any adverse criticism at work.

MANAGEMENT STRATEGY

When it comes to working out a strategy for coping with a trauma at work, managers should study the problems carefully.

If we take the case of a bank, we can see that there is an inherent risk involved no matter how carefully the bank organizes its security. There were bank raids long before Billy the Kid came along and a look at any newspaper shows that banks and other places where cash is regularly handled, such as post offices, are still being held up.

DIFFERENT EMPLOYEE RESPONSES

If a bank is robbed by armed men the experience is clearly very frightening for all concerned. But one employee may interpret the risk differently from another. One may say 'I thought that as long as we did what he said we'd be all right' while another might say, 'When he pulled out his gun, I was sure he was going to shoot us all. I knew I was going to die.'

DIFFERENT RESPONSES IN THE EMPLOYEES' HOMES

After the bank raid, the employees may go home and receive very different responses from their families. Some families may seek to make light of the incident, in order to help the victim to get over it; some may get anxious and demand that the employee leave and go to a safer job; some husbands or wives may get angry on their spouse's behalf and vow revenge. According to the response the employee gets at home, he or she will return to work more or less able to cope the next day.

GETTING BACK TO NORMAL

If there has been a violent incident in the work-place, normal practices stop. Although everyone knows that eventually they will have to start up again, the routine has been broken and not only do employees want to talk about the traumatic incident, but they also feel that now is the opportunity to raise other grievances that have lain dormant for some time.

As the place gets back to normal, some employees will have adjusted quicker than others, and those who are slow to adjust may be resented by the rest as being weak or even malingering to get out of their share of the work or else to attract attention. Without any kind of help or counselling, the situation is unlikely to improve.

Few people are naturally litigious, and it usually takes a lot for someone to decide to go ahead and sue his or her employer. When they do so, it is often as a result of feeling that no one in the company has taken their suffering seriously. When asked what tipped them over the edge into filing a law suit, a significant number of employees said that they had felt abandoned by their bosses.

NIPPING PTSD IN THE BUD

If the management of every company were to provide this book for all employees, they would be doing themselves a favour. Where the company is not big enough to warrant taking on a full-time trauma specialist, as some American firms have done, it can at least train its management to cope with a crisis and can have contingency plans for dealing with employees who have undergone a traumatic experience and who may go on to develop PTSD unless they are given the appropriate treatment at the time.

Assessment at an early stage to see how badly affected the employees are (the same day or the following morning at the latest) should be the first action taken. Where a number of people were involved, group debriefings may help. When those people most severely affected are pinpointed, the management should consider the options according to how each person's condition goes. If the person's well-being seems to be threatened, the management should encourage the employee to go for treatment – and in most cases this will be covered by the company's insurance or compensation funding. No employer wants to end up with someone suffering from PTSD.

INTERVENTION BY VICTIM SUPPORT

Victim Support has been concerned at the lack of support many employers give their staff following crime at their place of work. In 1990, they held a seminar for employers and trade-unionists from commercial and public sector organizations in order to raise the issue and to encourage companies to improve the level of care they are prepared to offer.

The Princess Royal, patron of the scheme, addressed the seminar, which was attended by over 150 employers, and the meeting was also addressed by the Home Secretary and experts from the Trades Union Congress and the commercial sector. Many companies admitted that in the past they had been thinking only about crime prevention at work; now they would actively consider ways of assisting their employees in the aftermath of crime at work.

PTSD AND THE FAMILY

There is no doubt that PTSD can transform a loving spouse and parent into someone who seems like a stranger. During the flashbacks, the trauma – whatever it happens to be – is as real to the sufferer of this illness as when it happened. The real world around is not the place it used to be – the trauma has contaminated it. And added to the fear and anxiety brought on by the original incident or series of incidents is the knowledge the sufferer has that he or she is behaving in a strange way. The trap is that the victim just cannot help it. Try as they might, victims cannot escape the trap and, like rats in a cage, they can turn on others or inflict more damage on themselves.

PTSD can be helped – it can be overcome by the technique I have described in this book. But, until sufferers have mastered the disorder, a lot of damage may have been done – not only to themselves but especially to their most important family relationships.

The family of someone suffering from PTSD will have had to stand by helpless as the person they love twists and turns in a torment of frustration. No amount of counselling is going to help someone get rid of those intrusive images. Perhaps after many years the symptoms will have subsided, but those flashbacks, those hallucinations that the whole thing is happening again, can be reawakened by a chance remark or some other reminder which triggers off the reaction.

Tom Williams, a psychiatrist who has an interest in PTSD, tells a story which illustrates how trouble can lie dormant for years. One Christmas, he gave his father a book on the Battle of Okinawa. During the night he heard someone moving around and when he went down to the kitchen he found his father there, crying. He was saying to himself, 'We should never have made that night attack.' When he saw his son, he said angrily, 'Here's your damned book. It brought the nightmares back.'

If a memory which has been covered over by decades of trying to forget it can have such a powerful effect, then it is easy to see how a recent trauma can transform someone. However, it is very hard to remain loving, understanding and forgiving day after day. There are very few saints in the world, and most people find that their sympathy starts to run out after a while. Of course, this feeling of impatience and annoyance makes them ashamed. How could they be so cruel after all Tom, Dick or Harry has gone through? They make an effort to renew their sympathy and patience, but they have needs, too, which are no longer being met.

Let us take a concrete example.

Think of the case of a driver who has been so badly affected by an accident he has been involved in that he develops PTSD. We'll call him Mr Lee. He was not badly injured physically, but he was shaken up. When he gets home, his wife is very concerned and his children are told that Daddy is not very well and he mustn't be bothered. For a few days this situation continues, but it soon becomes clear that he is not making progress. If anything, he is getting worse.

Mrs Lee finds the changes in her husband quite disturbing. He wants to talk about nothing but the accident and he endlessly blames himself for not having done something to prevent it. He cannot sleep at night, he breaks into a sweat and he complains of palpitations. No matter how tempting the meals she makes, he is inclined to push them away after a few mouthfuls and he seems to be drinking more than he used to.

The children are bewildered. Their father doesn't seem to love them any more. He hardly talks to them unless it's to shout at them for something. He is much more irritable than he used to be and little things annoy him now that never worried him before the accident.

Apart from his increased irritability and a tendency to jump at the slightest noise, Mr Lee is apathetic. He can't seem to get interested in anything and, no matter what he is offered by way of amusement or distraction, he cannot raise the energy to take it up. His sex life with his wife is non-existent and this is half a sorrow and half a relief to Mrs Lee, because she is now beginning to feel that this is not the man she married.

Because the cause of the trauma was a traffic accident, Mr Lee is unable to drive the family car and this means that Mrs Lee has to drive everywhere. She has a part-time job and so this is an extra burden on her. In fact, she can no longer count on any help in the house from her husband and the children are more difficult to cope with because of the unhappy atmosphere at home.

In the end, she talks to a woman friend about it and says she is near the end of her tether. She decides she will have to confront him: either he pulls himself together by himself or he goes to see his doctor – that is her ultimatum. He gets very angry at what he sees as her goading him and this anger is fuelled by a guilty feeling that he has been difficult at home. A row starts and before he knows it he has hit her – something he has never done in all their married life.

She tells him to get out of the house and not to try to see her or the children until he can control himself.

This is not a true story, but it might just as well

be. It shows the disastrous road a relationship can take when someone is suffering from PTSD.

Dr Zahava Solomon, head of the research branch of the Israeli Defense Forces Mental Health Department, wrote a paper for the journal *Psychiatry* in August 1988 which examined the effect combat-related PTSD had on the family. 'Little attention has been paid to the disorder's potentially detrimental effects on veterans' families. The toll of war on women and children is immense' he concluded.

Because taking part in combat is just about the most stressful situation people can get themselves into, it is not surprising to find high levels of disturbance in soldiers once a war is over. Not only are soldiers in constant danger of being killed or injured, they are usually living in great discomfort with none of the familiar surroundings of their own private lives and far from their loved ones.

Combat stress can result in a condition known as CSR (combat stress reaction) which endures as long as the soldier is in the line of fire. The more serious condition is PTSD, which carries on after the war has ended. Some of the symptoms are shared by both disorders, but the crucial difference is that in PTSD the victim goes on living the trauma in his daily life.

While the combatants are away, the family is left at home to cope in the best way it can. The family not only has to get by without someone who may have been the breadwinner, it is also constantly anxious about whether the loved one is still alive and well. In modern times, the huge escalation in the amount of media coverage given to a war means that there are constant reminders of the situation and nerves can be stretched to breaking point. And yet the soldier seldom has much contact with home while the war is on — maybe just the odd letter.

Not only do the members of the family (and this applies to the extended family, too) swing between hope and despair, they have also had to make new arrangements at home in the absence of the member who has gone away.

Since in most cases we are talking of the husband and father who has gone to war and the wife and children who have stayed at home, we can see that the woman will have had to take over certain roles that her husband previously fulfilled. She will have had to start taking the decisions and the children will have started taking on more responsibilities. After a time, people start to feel natural in these new roles and so, when the man of the house comes home and wants things to be just as they were before, it is not easy to do.

The soldier returning home may find his wife more assertive and independent and this will be hard for him to adjust to. For the soldier with PTSD, the problems will be multiplied. In a 1970 study of 200 Vietnam veterans who received treatment for PTSD, it was found that a high percentage suffered from severe interpersonal problems, especially in their marriages. Veterans who continue to mourn the deaths of those who were close to them in the army or who feel guilty that they survived when others didn't are often unable to maintain close personal relationships.

Not only does the wife of the veteran suffering from PTSD feel rejected emotionally, she is often rejected sexually as the man's interest in sexual relations is frequently diminished. This can lead to frustration and may even tempt a wife to look for a lover.

Coming straight from a situation where aggression was expected, it is understandable if the returned soldier has increased levels of aggression at home. He may be angry with himself, and his wife and children take a share of that anger and guilt. He may be unable to get the right balance when it comes to dealing with his young children. Any growing child will let off steam physically and a parent may sometimes need to check the amount of aggressiveness he or she displays. But someone suffering from PTSD is not fully in control and his attempts to deal with a child can get out of hand. This leads to fear and anger in a home which already has more than its share of tension.

A study conducted in 1980 found that 50 per cent of couples who went for counselling reported wife battering. It was not the type of wife battering found in the population at large, but arose on one or two occasions only, when the situation got dramatically out of hand. The man had been as horrified as the woman when the air had cleared, and some good may even have come from it, because it was usually the spur the couple needed to go and seek professional help.

The children of PTSD veterans experience 'considerable distress, depression and self-doubts' and may feel guilty themselves. In playing with other children, they may get unduly aggressive or they may go out looking for a fight in order to show that they can do what their fathers have done.

Unfortunately, unless help is sought quickly enough and is effective rapidly enough the situation deteriorates and it has been proved that as many as 38 per cent of the marriages of Vietnam veterans broke up within six months of their return from South-East Asia.

Even if the marriage does not end in divorce, it may survive only at the expense of the wife's well-being. She may have to take on far more than her share of the duties within the marriage and also cope with a husband who stretches her resources to the limit. She may be caught in the 'compassion trap', in which she makes too many sacrifices for other people and does not allow herself to express any anger or resentment. In time, holding it all back is no longer possible, and she may lash out at her children or lapse into depression.

What is true of the wives of PTSD veterans is just as true for the wives of civilians suffering from the illness. The strain will ultimately be too much for even the strongest marriage if no light can be seen at the end of the tunnel.

THE ROAD BACK

By the time you read this chapter, you may already have got out of the trap. If you have, or someone close to you has, you will know that now is the time to rebuild close family ties. All the members of the family, who have had such an anxious and unhappy time, are also freed from the trap and you may experience stronger bonds than you had before the illness. You will have gone through an ordeal together and come out the other side. That is one of the strongest bonds there is.

11

COUNSELLORS

Counsellors are often among the very first people that victims of a disaster turn to. It may be a disaster on the large scale, such as at Lockerbie, where PanAm Flight 103 exploded in mid-air, or a disaster only for the person concerned. In either case, the victim is in a sort of mental agony and is looking for a way to ease the pain. Unless you are very careful, they could pass on their own anguish to you.

Counsellors are particularly vulnerable and liable to become victims of PTSD. This is because the people they counsel are likely to unload in great detail the events of the traumatic episode they have lived through. Some counsellors can take it, but others can't. Who do *they* unload it all on? Who could they possibly tell such gruesome details to? Most probably, nobody.

The British Psychological Society has clearly

expressed its concern about counsellors. In its circular 'Psychological Aspects of Disaster', published in September 1990, it recommends that counsellors should be supervised. (Every counsellor should read this circular. Copies can be obtained from The British Psychological Society, St Andrews House, 48 Princess Road East, Leicester LE1 7DR – telephone 0533-549568.) Supervision, however, is not going to get rid of the recurring images once they have set in.

RECOMMENDATIONS

There are two things I would recommend counsellors to do.

HELPING YOUR CLIENT

If you are a counsellor meeting a client for the first time, just obtain a brief statement about what the problem is – for example, your client may have been viciously assaulted or involved in a major accident. Then proceed to find out what is disturbing your client most. Are you dealing with a case of PTSD? Is his or her life being cut through by recurring images and the other symptoms?

If so, immediately offer the rewind technique

described in Chapter 7. Explain that the technique will allow him or her to get rid of intrusive images that come flooding back at any time of the day or night, causing dread and anxiety. It will *not* wipe out the memories – the patient will always be able to recall what happened – but it will put the patient in the driving seat. He or she will be able to recall the events at will, and will no longer have the sense of living in a nightmare world.

In this way, your client will be spared the necessity of recounting the whole traumatic event, which is bound to upset him or her, and **you will be spared the full details**.

Review your client in a week. You will find that he or she is now out of the trap, freed from recurring images and ready to find ways forward with your assistance. Don't forget, however, that there may be other images which had been lying dormant and which now have the opportunity to surface. Ask whether any of these previously suppressed images have now come to the surface, reassure the client that this is perfectly normal, and treat these images in turn with the rewind technique.

TREATING YOURSELF

If you feel you can no longer endure giving support as you are weighed down by recurrent images passed on to you by listening to (and imagining) other people's traumatic events, then treat yourself.

TREATMENT FOR COUNSELLORS

Model your own treatment on that outlined in Chapter 7 for the rescuers, which starts on page 155. The main difference will be in the content. The rescuer actually arrived on the scene of the event, while you, the counsellor, will have heard an account of the event, from either a victim, a bystander or a rescuer. In some large-scale disasters you may even have had the story from all three sources.

If you in turn become a victim – if you start to experience recurring intrusive images based on what you have been told – then you need to rewind the sequence.

Do the rewind, get rid of the various images that you have stored and, in the future, treat PTSD victims as I suggest above. You will find your job far more rewarding and you will be able to deal with greater numbers of clients.

Here is a case history which illustrates how the sufferer found it an enormous relief not to have to relate in detail all the grim details of her particular trauma.

THE VICTIM OF INCEST
Denise Canning

This twenty-three-year-old woman came to seek help after having been forced to have an incestuous relationship with her brother over the past seven years. On leaving home she had suddenly become painfully aware that she had been living a distorted life and was riddled with a sense of guilt.

When she first arrived, she briefly outlined her problem and I reassured her that I did not want, or need, to know the details of her ordeal. This relieved her enormously, for she was already seeing a counsellor to whom she had painfully revealed many details. Ms Canning understood how the counsellor was trying to help, but she knew she wasn't actually being shown a way out of the trap.

Prior to the treatment, she was asked to fill in an IES (impact of events scale) questionnaire. The result gave a strong indication of PTSD. She explained in broad terms what was at the root of her disturbance. Her brother began approaching her when he was around sixteen with demands that she join him in various sexual activities. He used to threaten her both psychologically and physically if she resisted. Indeed, it was so much part of her early life that she came to accept it as normal.

When she realized that there was something really wrong with that way of life, she was invaded by guilty feelings. An immediate consequence was that she became very quiet and withdrawn. Socially, she would vary from being passive to suddenly talking too much and 'annoying everyone'.

She has no experience with boyfriends and, although her brother has since married, he is still seeking her sexual favours. She now refuses, but has a lot of anger and guilt inside her.

Ms Canning was very relaxed after discovering that she didn't have to tell me any details so we proceeded straight to the rewind technique. She had some difficulty initially, but did it well the second time. She left, saying that she felt that the scenes she had just rewound appeared somewhat confused. This is a very typical response after doing the rewind if the patient is asked: 'How do you feel about your traumatic event if you think about it now, quickly?'

Two weeks later she returned to report on how she had got on. Her second IES questionnaire showed a great improvement.

Asked how she felt different, she said, 'It's not the kick in the teeth it was. It is more logical and I can think about it without getting too tied up.'

Interestingly, when she got home she tried out the rewind on one particular recurring image which she had been troubled by and which she wanted to go through on her own, an image which had been 'popping up and kicking me in the face'. She also explained that now when she goes to bed 'I lie there thinking, but not in the same way. It has lifted a space for me to know how to deal with other images.'

SPEED IS OF THE ESSENCE

Use the rewind technique on your client as soon as possible, because there is a high incidence of drop-out for those in therapy. A client may only come once or twice and then feel there is no point and miss future appointments. Take the opportunity to treat the person as soon as you can, rather than let him or her go off with the impression that therapy has failed them, feeling more isolated than before.

An American study reported that with patients who entered treatment for PTSD during the first nine weeks after the trauma the dropout rate was 26.9 per cent. Where patients entered treatment forty weeks or more after the original trauma, the drop-out rate was 81.8 per cent.

WHY DO PATIENTS DROP OUT OF TREATMENT?

There are no hard and fast rules, but I can think of some probable reasons. Patients who have already tried other forms of treatment and who were disappointed by them arrive expecting to be disappointed; if there are no instant results, they don't see the point of continuing. Another group of early drop-outs might be the people who hope to get compensation for their illness and who do not want to jeopardize their chances of an award by appearing to be perfectly well again.

12

CONCLUSION

It is my earnest hope that this book will have done for my readers what I have been able to do for patients who have come to me for treatment – open the trauma trap. Until the victim of PTSD is actually out of that trap nothing else will have a chance of getting through. You may be able to look through the glass walls of a trap and see that there is a big wide world out there but it is of no use unless you can get into it. Running in circles, ever afraid that the nightmare will come back, is no way of living and the suffering means that you are likely to become worn down and prey to other disorders.

Very often, insensitive media coverage of disasters, both large-scale and small, means that the victims of PTSD are painfully reminded of a trauma just when they are least expecting it. The press and television coverage is understandable, but the images are often grossly intrusive and can serve no purpose other than to shock. The media often resurrect the whole affair when the anniversary comes round or at the time of an inquest or enquiry. I should like to make a plea to media editors and producers to show greater restraint when they cover stories where people have been involved in trauma. Their irresponsible attitudes can mean devastating hurt to those who have been hurt enough.

There are some people who may be reading this book who have not suffered from PTSD themselves yet who fall into the group of nearly-theres. These are the people who by sheer chance or by some unexplained premonition were not where they were supposed to be when a disaster took place. There are people walking around today who failed to take their places on a plane or a train which subsequently crashed. There are others who would normally have been in a place where a violent crime was committed, such as the bank teller who was absent from work on the day the bank was raided. These and people in other sets of circumstances may well feel: 'There but for the grace of God go I.'

I give this instance because amongst the nearly-there's a few may have actually been quite upset for a long time. Technically, however, they are not at present classified as suffering from PTSD.

There are, naturally, grey areas in dealing with matters which concern the human mind. Other events can cause intense anxiety and grief but cannot be classed strictly as events likely to cause PTSD. I do not wish to extend the definition of the disorder, but I recognize that when we are dealing with something like PTSD there will be some uncertainties. I am quite sure, however, that some positive steps should be taken at once to help people in great distress. If the disorder is stress or anxiety, that is serious enough and those who feel that they are in need of outside help should contact their family doctor or one of the organizations listed in Chapter 9.

I should like to say a word or two about soldiers, who run a high risk of becoming victims of PTSD. Hugh McManners, the Commando captain during the Falklands campaign who is quoted in Chapter 2, believes that although they are not visible, like having a leg blown off, the numbers of psychiatric injuries in modern warfare are very great. He estimates them to amount to nearly a third of the number actually wounded. Moreover, he predicts that 'the Gulf war will create a surge of much younger people who will require care over the next decade or more'. We must all hope that the skills to treat these victims will become widely disseminated, so that a lot of needless suffering can be cut out.

The levels of understanding of PTSD are growing all the time although there is, unfortunately, still a long way to go. Tom Howard, the Falklands soldier whose symptoms are almost like a textbook example of the disorder, went to see a psychiatrist and became enraged at the diagnosis that was made. He was told: 'You have an immature personality. You should go away and pull yourself together.' If you are unlucky enough to come across a professional who has never heard of PTSD, you might suggest that he or she should read this book.

But, if you have reached the concluding chapter, it probably means that you have understood what the illness is and gone on to treat yourself or helped someone else to do so. I believe that the treatment is one which can transform lives and that is why I want it to be available to everyone straight away. If you have been through the rewind and it has worked for you, let other people know. You may be acquainted with fellow sufferers who have never admitted their problem to you or who are not even aware of it themselves. Hearing of your experience may give them the courage to offer themselves an escape from the trap and a chance to start living life as it should be lived.

INDEX